CHRISTMAS COOKBOOK

With Pictures Quick & Easy Holiday Dessert Recipes Cookbook

(The Ultimate Christmas Cookie Recipes Collection!)

Alfred Steele

Published by Alex Howard

© **Alfred Steele**

All Rights Reserved

Christmas Cookbook: With Pictures Quick & Easy Holiday Dessert Recipes Cookbook (The Ultimate Christmas Cookie Recipes Collection!)

ISBN 978-1-990169-56-4

All rights reserved. No part of this guide may be reproduced in any form without permission in writing from the publisher except in the case of brief quotations embodied in critical articles or reviews.

Legal & Disclaimer

The information contained in this book is not designed to replace or take the place of any form of medicine or professional medical advice. The information in this book has been provided for educational and entertainment purposes only.

The information contained in this book has been compiled from sources deemed reliable, and it is accurate to the best of the Author's knowledge; however, the Author cannot guarantee its accuracy and validity and cannot be held liable for any errors or omissions. Changes are periodically made to this book. You must consult your doctor or get professional medical advice before using any of the suggested remedies, techniques, or information in this book.

Table of contents

Part 1 1

1. Biscuits Decorated With Christmas 2

2. Christmas Log Ice Cream With Chocolate Butter 5

3. Cupcake My Darling 9

4. Coffee Cupcakes 12

5. Chocolate And Mint Cupcakes............................... 15

6. Dark Chocolate Cupcakes With Peanut Butter...... 19

7. Chocolate And Pistachio Cupcakes 24

8. Chocolate Cupcakes With Almond And Nougat Flavors 29

9. Cranberry Cupcakes 32

10. Cupcakes With Matcha Tea And Honey............... 35

11. Thermomix Fruit Christmas Log............................ 38

12. Christmas Log With Passion Fruit 41

13. Log Of The Tropics 46

14. Christmas Cookies With Hazelnuts 52

15. Frozen Christmas Cookies 54

16. Wolf Tooth Biscuits 59

17. Spoon Cookies Truffle With Chocolate 61

18. Christmas Cookies With Spices... 66

19. Chilled Strawberry, Vanilla And Chocolate Log 69

20. Nougatine Ice Cream Log 73

21. Chilled Cookie Log.. 77

22. Ice-Cream Log With Raspberry 82

23. Light Log With Mango 86

24. Light Chocolate Log 89

25. Raspberry Mousse Log 92

26. Log Walnuts Strudel Way 94

27. Brownie With Walnut Kernels 97

28. Vanilla Brownie 100

29. Cheesecake With Cookies 102

30. Biscuits With Orange...105

31. Cornets Of Beggar Pancakes..107

32. Cream Cheese And Cream Of Chestnut 110

33. Homemade Apple Crumble And Homemade Chestnut Cream 111

34. Fondant With Chocolate And Brown Cream 113

35. Chocolate Cake With Raspberry 115

36. Dark Chocolate Crepe Cake 119

37. Christmas Cake (Christmas Cake) 121

38. Lemon And Yogurt Ice Cream 125

39. Layer Cake With Macaroons 127

40. Layer Chocolate Cheesecake, Ferrero® And Nutella® 130

Part 2 136

Main Course 137

Sunday Rib Roast 137

Breakfast Casserole 138

Christmas Roast Duck With Crispy Potatoes 141

Whole Baked Salmon In Recipies Salt 145

Vegan Mushroom, Chestnut & Cranberry Tart 147

Persian Squash & Pistachio Roast 150

Prime Rib 155

Christmas Recipies 156

Cauliflower & Broccoli Cheese 156

Maple Roast Turkey And Gravy 159

Duck Breasts Stuffed With Sugared Nuts 162

Honey Glazed Ham 164

Christmas Tortellini & Spinach Soup 166

Christmas Eve Confetti Pasta 167

Chicken Wild Rice Soup 169

Creamy Seafood-Stuffed Shells 170

Ultimate Roast Chicken 172

Italian Style Pizza 174

Mexican Sweetcorn Pancakes, Poached Eggs And Salsa 176

Mushroom Purses 178

Cakes & Bakery 180

Gingerbread Men 180

Stollen Muffins 183

Homemade Crumpets With Burnt Honey Butter 185

Candy Cane Cookies 186

Part 1

1. Biscuits Decorated With Christmas

PREPARATION GUIDE: BISCUITS DECORATED WITH CHRISTMAS

- Number of persons: 20 Pers.
- Preparation time: 10 minutes
- Cooking time: 15 min
- Rest: 1 h
- Recipe cost: Cheap
- Difficulty: Easy

INGREDIENTS

Biscuits:

- 100 grams butter

- 150 grams Granulated sugar

- 1 egg

- 1 small pinch of salt

- 260 grams flour

- The zest of a lemon

Royal icing:

- 2 egg whites

- 2 teaspoon lemon juice

- 400 grams of icing sugar

PREPARATION

STEP 1

Prepare the cookies.

2ND STEP

In a bowl, cream butter, sugar and salt together with a whisk.

STEP 3

Add the lemon zest.

STEP 4

Stir in the flour.

STEP 5

Cover the paste with food film and reserve in the refrigerator for about 1 hour.

STEP 6

Preheat your oven to 180 ° C.

STEP 7

On a floured worktop, spread out your pastry on 0,5mm.

STEP 8

Cut out with pieces of the shape of your choice.

STEP 9

Bake for about 12min.

STEP 10

At the exit of the oven, let cool a little before taking off.

STEP 11

Prepare the royal icing.

STEP 12

Whip egg whites and lemon juice.

STEP 13

As soon as they start to become sparkling and white, add the icing sugar and whip energetically.

STEP 14

Divide into bowls to color and pour into sockets.

STEP 15

Decorate the cookies.

STEP 16

Once your shortbread is cold, decorate them as you please, giving free rein to your imagination.

STEP 17

Let dry about 5h to 6h.

STEP 18

Keep in an airtight box.

2. Christmas Log Ice Cream With Chocolate Butter

PREPARATION GUIDE CHOCOLATE BUTTER CHRISTMAS ICE CHOKE

- Number of persons: 8 Pers.
- Preparation time: 30 min
- Cooking time: 10 minutes
- Rest: 10 minutes
- Difficulty: Easy

INGREDIENTS

For the cake

- 5 whole eggs

- 250g of flour

- 250 g of sugar

- 5 g of baking powder

- 2 g of salt

-To stick the logs

- 1 egg white

- 4 tablespoons icing sugar

- For butter and chocolate icing

- 875 g icing sugar

- 125 g unsweetened cocoa

- 85 ml of milk

- 5 ml of vanilla essence

- 125 g of soft butter

PREPARATION

STEP 1

Preheat the oven to th.6 (180ºC).

2ND STEP

Beat the eggs at high speed and gradually add the sugar. Beat until the mixture is thick.

STEP 3

Mix the dry ingredients together and add them in small amounts by gently lifting the mixture with a spatula.

STEP 4

Prepare a greased rectangular plate, cover it with baking paper and spread the dough evenly over the plate. Bake for 10 minutes.

STEP 5

On leaving the oven, immediately return to a damp cloth and roll. Let stand 5 to 10 minutes. Unwrap and coat with apple jelly, then roll again.

STEP 6

Take two or three slices of roll about 5 cm thick.

STEP 7

In a bowl, mix the icing sugar and the egg whites. Brush the areas of the log where you want to stick the logs and glue the slices of logs. Keep the time that the glue takes. If needed, plant a wooden skewer for drying. Book 30 minutes cool.

STEP 8

For the frosting, whip the butter in the ointment, add the icing sugar with the cocoa alternating with the milk, and then add the vanilla.

STEP 9

Spread on the cake well chilled with a spatula. Draw streaks with a fork to simulate the wood.

STEP 10

Decorate with almond paste leaves, sugar stars, dark chocolate shavings, or sprinkle with a little icing sugar to give the effect of snow.

3. Cupcake My Darling

PREPARATION GUIDE CUPCAKE MY CHER

- Number of persons: 6 Pers.
- Preparation time:30 min
- Cooking time: 20 min
- Rest: 15 min
- Difficulty: Easy

INGREDIENTS

- 1 egg

- 83 ml of butter

- 83 ml of powdered sugar

- 42 ml of milk

- 125 ml of flour

- 2 ml of baking powder

- 20 ml of cocoa

- 5 ml of kirsch

-For the frosting

- 6 My dear

- 4 drops of red dye

- 83 ml icing sugar

- 83 ml of butter

- 5 ml of kirsch

PREPARATION

STEP 1

Preheat your oven th.5 6 (160 ° C).

2ND STEP

Place the My Darling in the freezer.

STEP 3

Beat the egg, add the sugar and whiten it. Add the softened butter and stir until you get a light texture.

STEP 4

Add flour and sifted yeast, mix, add milk, kirsch and then cocoa.

STEP 5

Mix well to obtain a creamy texture.

STEP 6

Divide the preparation into the muffin cups and bake for 15 to 22 minutes until they are puffy and firm to the touch.

STEP 7

Meanwhile prepare the frosting

STEP 8

Beat the butter and sugar to a fluffy texture. Add the dye and kirsch and whip the mixture with the electric whisk.

STEP 9

Reserve in a pastry bag and place in the fridge.

STEP 10

Once the cupcakes are cooked, let them cool completely then make a hole in their centers and insert a darling; to finish, cover with frosting.

4. Coffee Cupcakes

PREPARATION GUIDE COFFEE CUPCAKES

- Number of persons: 6 Pers.
- Preparation time: 30 min
- Cooking time: 20 min
- Difficulty: Easy

INGREDIENTS

For cakes

- 200 g flour

- 1 cup of espresso coffee

- 300 g caster sugar

- 4 whole eggs

- 250 g of soft butter

- 1 teaspoon of liquid vanilla extract

- 1 teaspoon of baking powder

- 1 pinch of salt

For icing

- 250 g of soft butter

- 400 g icing sugar

- 1 teaspoon of liquid coffee extracts

PREPARATION

STEP 1

Prepare the cakes

2ND STEP

Preheat the oven to 180 ° C or the 6.

STEP 3

Place paper boxes in muffin pans.

STEP 4

In a bowl, whisk the soft butter with the caster sugar and the liquid vanilla extract using an electric mixer.

STEP 5

Add the whole eggs and mix with the mixer.

STEP 6

Then add the flour, salt and baking powder and espresso coffee. Mix with a spoon to obtain a smooth and homogeneous paste.

STEP 7

Pour the dough into the paper boxes until 2⁄3.

STEP 8

Bake in the preheated oven and cook for 20 minutes.

STEP 9

At the end of the oven, let the cakes cool on a rack, then unmold them.

STEP 10

In the meantime, prepare the frosting

STEP 11

In a bowl, beat the soft butter with the icing sugar and the liquid coffee extract, using an electric mixer, until obtaining a smooth and homogeneous cream.

STEP 12

Place frosting until cool.

STEP 13

When the cakes have cooled, remove the frosting from the cool and place it in a pastry bag.

STEP 14

Put it nicely on the cakes, then keep the cupcakes cool until tasting.

STEP 15

Take these cupcakes out of the fridge 10 minutes before savoring them.

5. Chocolate And Mint Cupcakes

PREPARATION GUIDE CHOCOLATE AND MINT CUPCAKES

- Number of persons: 6 Pers.
- Preparation time: 35 min
- Cooking time: 20 min
- Difficulty: Easy

INGREDIENTS

For cakes

- 100 g of dark chocolate to bake

- 120 g of flour

- 70 g caster sugar

- 2 whole eggs

- 80 g of soft butter

- 1 teaspoon of baking powder

- 1 pinch of salt

For icing

- 250 g of soft butter

- 400 g icing sugar

- 2 teaspoons liquid mint extract

- a few drops of blue food coloring

PREPARATION

STEP 1

Prepare the cakes

2ND STEP

Preheat the oven to 180 ° C or the 6.

STEP 3

Place paper boxes in muffin pans.

STEP 4

In a bowl, beat the whole eggs with the powdered sugar until the mixture whitens.

STEP 5

Melt the dark chocolate cut into pieces with the butter in a bowl in the microwave.

STEP 6

Add it to the previous preparation and stir well.

STEP 7

Then add the flour, salt and baking powder. Mix with a spoon to obtain a smooth and homogeneous paste.

STEP 8

Pour the dough into the paper boxes until 2³.

STEP 9

Bake in the preheated oven and cook for 20 to 25 minutes depending on the size of the cakes.

STEP 10

At the end of the oven, let the cakes cool on a rack, then unmold them.

STEP 11

In the meantime, prepare the frosting

STEP 12

In a bowl, beat the soft butter with the icing sugar and liquid mint extract, using an electric mixer, until you obtain a smooth and homogeneous cream.

STEP 13

Add a few drops of blue food coloring, depending on the color you want, and stir.

STEP 14

Place frosting until cool.

STEP 15

When the cakes have cooled, remove the frosting from the cool and place it in a pastry bag.

STEP 16

Put it nicely on the cakes, then keep the cupcakes cool until tasting.

STEP 17

Take out these dark chocolate and mint cupcakes for 10 minutes before savoring them.

6. Dark Chocolate Cupcakes With Peanut Butter

PREPARATION GUIDE BLACK CHOCOLATE CUPCAKES AND CACAHUÈTES BUTTER

- Number of persons: 12 Pers.
- Preparation time: 45 min
- Cooking time: 25 min
- Difficulty: Easy

INGREDIENTS

For cakes

- 100g of flour

- 75 g of dark chocolate to bake

- 175 g caster sugar

- 3 whole eggs

- 12 teaspoon baking powder

- 175 g of soft butter

- 2 tablespoons of milk

For icing

- 5 tablespoons peanut butter

- 45 ml of fresh cream

- 175 g icing sugar

- 120 g of brown sugar

- 40 g of soft butter

PREPARATION

STEP 1

Prepare the cakes

2ND STEP

Preheat the oven to 180 ° C or the 6.

STEP 3

Place paper boxes in muffin pans.

STEP 4

In a bowl, beat the whole eggs with the powdered sugar until the mixture whitens.

STEP 5

Melt the dark chocolate cut into pieces with the butter in a bowl in the microwave.

STEP 6

Add it to the previous preparation and stir well.

STEP 7

Then add the flour, baking powder and milk. Mix with a spoon to obtain a smooth and homogeneous paste.

STEP 8

Pour the dough into the paper boxes until 23.

STEP 9

Bake in the preheated oven and cook for 20 minutes.

STEP 10

At the end of the oven, let the cakes cool on a rack, then unmold them.

STEP 11

In the meantime, prepare the frosting

STEP 12

Put the peanut butter, soft butter, caster sugar and liquid cream in a saucepan.

STEP 13

Place the pan over low heat and let the mixture warm, stirring well, until the sugar is completely dissolved.

STEP 14

Remove the pan from the heat, then add the icing sugar and stir until the mixture is smooth.

STEP 15

Let the glaze warm to room temperature, then cool until use.

STEP 16

When the cakes have cooled, remove the frosting from the cool and place it in a pastry bag.

STEP 17

Put it nicely on the cakes, then keep the cupcakes cool until tasting.

STEP 18

Take these chocolate and peanut butter cupcakes out of the fridge 10 min before serving.

7. Chocolate And Pistachio Cupcakes

PREPARATION GUIDE CHOCOLATE AND PISTACHIO CUPCAKES

- Number of persons: 6 Pers.
- Preparation time: 25 min
- Cooking time: 15 min
- Difficulty: Easy

INGREDIENTS

For the base

- 2 eggs

- 100 g caster sugar

- 115 g of butter

- 110 g chocolate 70% cocoa

- 20 g unsweetened cocoa powder

- 75 g flour

- 60 g of mascarpone

- 12 teaspoon of sodium bicarbonate

- 34 teaspoon baking powder

- salt

For the pistachio cream

- 50 g pistachio paste

- 150 g caster sugar

- 100 g of hot butter

- 100 g of ointment butter (to be incorporated cold)

- 60 g corn flour

- 50 cl of milk

- 50 g egg yolks

PREPARATION

STEP 1

Prepare the pistachio cream

2ND STEP

Garnish a dish with food film.

STEP 3

In a saucepan, heat the milk.

STEP 4

In a bowl, mix the eggs, sugar and whisk until the mixture is white.

STEP 5

Add the corn flour and reserve.

STEP 6

Weigh the butter hot, cut it into pieces and set aside.

STEP 7

Once the milk is hot, add the pistachio paste and mix.

STEP 8

Pour this mixture over the mixture of yolks while whisking.

STEP 9

Pour everything into the pan and place on medium heat. Whip until thickened and bubbling (you must keep boiling for at least 2 minutes).

STEP 10

Once the cream is ready, add the butter and mix well until it is melted.

STEP 11

Pour the cream into the mold covered with cling film, film again on contact and place in the freezer when it is completely cold. Then place it in the fridge while preparing the base.

STEP 12

Prepare the base

STEP 13

Preheat your oven to 180 ° C (th.6).

STEP 14

Melt the chocolate and butter in the microwave. Stir in the cocoa powder and let cool.

STEP 15

In a salad bowl, mix flour, baking soda, yeast and reserve.

STEP 16

In the bowl of a food processor, mix eggs, sugar, vanilla extract and salt.

STEP 17

Stir in the cooled chocolate mixture and half of the flour.

STEP 18

Add the mascarpone and the remaining flour while continuing to whisk.

STEP 19

Pour the dough into the molds and bake for 15 min. Let cool on a rack.

STEP 20

Cupcakes

STEP 21

Cut the ointment butter into pieces.

STEP 22

Microwave it to make it soft.

STEP 23

Put the custard in the bowl of a robot with the whisk and whip just to soften it.

STEP 24

Add the butter and whisk until it turns white and stays well.

STEP 25

Put it in a pastry bag and garnish the cupcakes.

STEP 26

Decorate them with some unsalted pistachio chips.

8. Chocolate Cupcakes With Almond And Nougat Flavors

PREPARATION GUIDE CHOCOLATE CUPCAKES TASTE ALMOND AND NOUGAT

- Number :10 muffins
- Preparation time: 10 minutes
- Cooking time: 10 minutes
- Difficulty: Easy

INGREDIENTS

- 60 g of flour

- 120 g chocolate 70% cocoa
- 15 g of almond powder
- 10 nougats
- 90 g of butter
- 80 g of sugar
- 3 eggs
- 1 packet of dry yeast
- -For the frosting
- 80 g of very soft butter
- 80 g icing sugar
- 1 teaspoon of peppermint extract
- 4 striped barley sugars

PREPARATION

STEP 1

Preheat the oven to 200 ° C (6-7).

2ND STEP

In a bowl beat the butter with icing sugar and peppermint extract. Book in the fridge.

STEP 3

Break the chocolate into pieces and melt in the microwave with the butter. Mix well.

STEP 4

In a bowl, whisk the eggs with the sugar. Add the chocolate-butter mixture.

STEP 5

Add the flour and half of the yeast packet. Mix thoroughly. Finally, add the almond powder and mix again until you obtain a homogeneous paste.

STEP 6

Divide into muffin cups and place a nougat in the center of each muffin. Bake for 10 minutes.

STEP 7

At the end of cooking, let cool. Roughly crush the barley sugars.

STEP 8

When the muffins are cold, decorate them with icing using a pastry bag and sprinkle with crushed barley sugars.

9. Cranberry Cupcakes

PREPARATION GUIDE CUPCAKES AT CRANBERRIES

- Number of persons: 8 Pers.
- Preparation time: 20 min
- Cooking time: 20 min
- Recipe cost: Cheap
- Difficulty: Easy

INGREDIENTS

For the cakes

- 120 g of flour

- 5 cl of milk

- 80 g of butter

- 80 g of sugar

- 2 eggs

- 12 teaspoon baking powder

For the topping

- 200 g of mascarpone

- 100 g icing sugar

- 1 handful of fresh cranberries

- 1 tablespoon of vanilla extract

PREPARATION

STEP 1

Prepare the cakes

2ND STEP

Preheat the oven to 180 ° C.

STEP 3

In a salad bowl, sift the flour and add the yeast. Mix.

STEP 4

In a bowl, stir the soft butter with the sugar and break the eggs and beat well.

STEP 5

Stir in the flour and add the milk and mix.

STEP 6

Pour the dough into cupcake trays and put in the oven for 20 minutes.

STEP 7

At the end of the oven, let cool to facilitate demolding.

STEP 8

Prepare the topping

STEP 9

Clean and blot cranberries.

STEP 10

Beat the mascarpone until you get a smooth cream.

STEP 11

Stir in the order icing sugar, cranberries and vanilla extract without stopping whipping.

STEP 12

Cover the cake with frosting using a pastry bag.

STEP 13

Serve.

10. Cupcakes With Matcha Tea And Honey

PREPARATION GUIDE MATCHA AND HONEY CUPCAKES

- Number of persons: 4 Pers.
- Preparation time: 10 minutes
- Cooking time: 12 min
- Difficulty: Easy

INGREDIENTS

- 100g of flour

- 1 teaspoon of yeast

- 70 g of butter

- 70 g of sugar

- 2 eggs

- 1 tablespoon acacia honey

- 1 teaspoon of MATCHA tea

- 1 pinch of salt

-For the frosting

- 150 g icing sugar

- 100 g of soft butter

- 1 teaspoon of MATCHA tea

- Sugar balls

PREPARATION

STEP 1

In a bowl, beat the soft butter with icing sugar and tea. Book fresh.

2ND STEP

Melt the honey with the butter over low heat or in the microwave. Add the MATCHA tea and mix until the mixture is homogeneous.

STEP 3

In a salad bowl, mix the flour, the yeast, the sugar and the pinch of salt. Add the eggs one by one and mix.

STEP 4

Pour the first mixture on the second. Mix intimately.

STEP 5

Pour into 12 muffin cups. Bake for 4 min at th.8 (240 ° C), then 6 to 8 min at th.7 (200 ° C).

STEP 6

The muffins should be golden brown. Check the cooking with a toothpick, which should come out dry. Let cool.

STEP 7

Once cold muffins, decorate with MATCHA frosting and sugar balls.

11. Thermomix Fruit Christmas Log

PREPARATION GUIDE CHRISTMAS LOGS WITH THERMOMIX FRUIT

- Number of persons: 6 Pers.
- Preparation time: 40 min
- Cooking time: 30 min
- Recipe cost: Cheap
- Difficulty: Easy

INGREDIENTS

- 300 g white chocolate

- 110 g flour

- 125 g cane sugar

- 4 eggs

- 250 ml of liquid cream

- 30 g of butter

- 12 mango

- 2 kiwis

- ½ glass of orange juice

PREPARATION

STEP 1

For the Genoese

2ND STEP

Install the whisk in the Thermomix. In the bowl, put the eggs and cane sugar and whisk for 6 min at speed 3 at 37 °. Then start again 6 min at speed 3, without temperature.

STEP 3

Add 110 g flour and whisk again for 4 seconds still at speed 3.

STEP 4

Arrange parchment paper on a baking sheet and spread the dough over it. Bake 7 min at th.6 (180 ° C). Let cool.

STEP 5

For the ganache

STEP 6

Cut the white chocolate into pieces and mix it with the Thermomix for 10 seconds at speed 10.

STEP 7

Add the cream and put the speed 3 at 50 °C for 4 min.

STEP 8

Add the butter and put the speed 3 at 50 °C for 1 min.

STEP 9

Let cool.

STEP 10

Reserve a quarter of the ganache. Peel kiwis and half mango and cut into small pieces. Stir in three-quarters of the chilled ganache. Stir well.

STEP 11

For assembly

STEP 12

Peel the sponge cake from the parchment paper. Soak it with orange juice with a brush.

STEP 13

Spread three quarters of the ganache on the sponge cake.

STEP 14

Roll the cake very gently to form a log.

STEP 15

Wrap the log in food film. Refrigerate for at least 12 hours.

STEP 16

For the final training

STEP 17

Just before the dessert, take out the log and cover it with the remaining ganache. Decorate, if you wish, with some slices of fruit placed on the log.

TIPS

You can vary the flavors in your Thermomix Fruit Christmas Log by adding various fruits to your taste, but be careful that they do not give too much juice (avoid citrus fruits for example).

12. Christmas Log With Passion Fruit

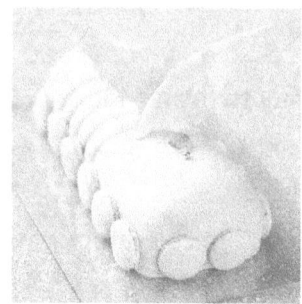

PREPARATION GUIDE CHRISTMAS LOG WITH FRUIT OF PASSION

- Number of persons: 8 Pers.
- Preparation time: 50 min
- Cooking time: 45 min
- Recipe cost: Cheap
- Difficulty: Intermediate

INGREDIENTS

- For the vanilla biscuit

- 3 egg whites

- 100 g of almond powder

- 100 g caster sugar

- 1 teaspoon of vanilla natural aroma extract.

For Bavarian passion fruit

- 20 passion fruits

- 4 egg yolks

- 100 g caster sugar

- 30 cl of milk

- 40 cl of whole liquid cream

- 3 sheets of edible gelatin

For the passion fruit insert

- 12 passion fruits

- 4 sheets of edible gelatin

- 1 teaspoon of liquid honey

For white chocolate icing

- 100 g of white chocolate

- 30 g icing sugar

- 20 g of butter

PREPARATION

STEP 1

Prepare the passion fruit insert. Soak the food gelatin sheets in a large bowl of cold water.

2ND STEP

Cut the passion fruit in half and get their juice. Mix and filter to remove the passion fruit seeds.

STEP 3

In a saucepan, bring the juice to a boil with the liquid honey. Let cool and add the dehydrated gelatin leaves. Mix to dissolve them well. Garnish your insert mold with passion fruit juice and let it freeze for at least 3 hours.

STEP 4

Preheat the oven to 180 ° C (thermostat 6). With an electric mixer, put the egg whites into firm snow. Gradually add the powdered sugar and vanilla natural flavor extract, while continuing to beat with a whisk. Pour the almond powder and mix the dough delicately with a spatula by lifting it well so as not to break the whites.

STEP 5

Pour the vanilla cookie dough on a baking sheet covered with parchment paper. Bake the biscuit for 15 minutes and remove from the oven. Let it cool before cutting it carefully to the size of your log mold.

STEP 6

Make the Bavarian with passion fruit. Soak the food gelatin sheets in a bowl of cold water.

STEP 7

Cut the fruit in half and get their juice. Filter well to remove all seeds.

STEP 8

In a bowl, beat the egg yolks with the powdered sugar until the mixture whitens.

STEP 9

In a saucepan, boil the milk with the liquid cream. In the first bouillon, pour over the egg yolks by whisking vigorously with a whisk. Put everything back in the pan and thicken, stirring regularly. Stir in passion fruit juice and continue cooking for 5 minutes. Warm up the preparation and add the dehydrated gelatin leaves. Mix well to dissolve and cool.

STEP 10

Make the Christmas log with passion fruit. Pour the Bavarian into the log mold. Position the passion fruit insert by pressing lightly to push in and cover with Bavarian. Cover with the vanilla biscuit. Reserve the Christmas dessert in the fridge for at least 4 hours.

STEP 11

Make the white chocolate icing that will come to coat your passion fruit Christmas log. Break the white chocolate into pieces and cut the butter into cubes. Melt everything in a bain-marie with the icing sugar. Stir with a wooden spoon until you get a smooth cream. Let the white chocolate frosting cool.

STEP 12

Take the opportunity to unmold your Christmas log with passion fruit. Pour the frosting on the Christmas log to coat it. Then keep it in the fridge for at least 1 hour before serving.

TIPS

For the release of your log, you can help a hair dryer to facilitate the takeoff of the walls of the mold.

13. Log Of The Tropics

PREPARATION GUIDE TROPICAL LOG

- Number of persons: 8 Pers.
- Preparation time: 1 h
- Cooking time: 10 minutes
- Difficulty: Intermediate

INGREDIENTS

For the biscuit

- 100 g white wheat flour, type 45

- 100 g caster sugar

- 4 eggs

- 1 tablespoon shaved with cinnamon

- 1 pinch of salt

For the foam

- 12 l of milk

- 100 g grated coconut

- 3 egg yolks

- 70 g caster sugar

- 1.5 dl liquid cream, very cold

- 4 sheets of gelatin

For the syrup

- 3 tablespoons of kirsch or white rum

- 1 tablespoon of sugar

For the decor

- 1 tablespoon acacia honey

- 40 g of blanched pistachios, or coconut powder, or cocoa powder ...

For the grout

- 400 g raspberries

- 50 g caster sugar

For coconut milk

- 12 l of milk

- 100 g grated coconut

PREPARATION

STEP 1

Twelve hours before preparing the log, prepare the coconut milk.

2ND STEP

Pour the milk into a saucepan and bring to a boil. Add the coconut and as soon as the boiling starts, remove from heat, mix, cover and let infuse.

STEP 3

Twelve hours later, prepare the dough.

STEP 4

Turn on the oven th.7 (225ºC). Cover a 30 cm x 40 cm baking sheet with parchment paper.

STEP 5

Break the eggs by separating the whites from the yolks. Put the whites in a large bowl and sprinkle with salt.

STEP 6

Put the yolks in a terrine, add the sugar and mix until the mixture whitens. Then add the flour and cinnamon sieving.

STEP 7

Whip the egg whites into the snow and add to the previous preparation, lifting with a spatula. Pour the dough on the plate and bake for 10 minutes.

STEP 8

Meanwhile, wet a towel, wring it out and spread it on the worktop. When the cookie is cooked, turn it over the wet cloth and remove the parchment paper. Roll together, squeezing the biscuit and the cloth tightly, starting at the small side of the rectangle. Let cool for at least 1 hour.

STEP 9

Prepare the mousse.

STEP 10

Filter the coconut milk and reserve the grated coconut. Pour the coconut milk (¼ liter remaining) in a saucepan and bring to a boil.

STEP 11

Put the gelatin sheets in a bowl of cold water. Let them soften.

STEP 12

Put the egg yolks in a saucepan, add the sugar and beat until the mixture whitens.

STEP 13

Pour the coconut milk in a thin stream, without stop whipping, then put the pan over low heat. Cook this custard, stirring constantly, until it coats the spatula.

STEP 14

Remove the pan from the heat, add the gelatin leaves by draining and mixing, they melt immediately in the heat.

STEP 15

Let the cream cool, turning it occasionally, then refrigerate until it begins to set.

STEP 16

When the custard begins to set, remove it from the refrigerator. Whip the liquid cream until it is firm and gently add it to the custard. Put in the refrigerator and let stand for 1 hour.

STEP 17

Prepare the cake assembly.

STEP 18

Prepare the syrup by mixing the sugar, the chosen alcohol and 1 dl of water, until the sugar melts. Unroll the biscuit on the cloth and moisten it with syrup.

STEP 19

Spread the mousse on the dough, then roll the biscuit, enclosing the foam.

STEP 20

Enclose the filled biscuit in a sheet of cling film and put it in the refrigerator. Let it sit for at least 12 hours.

STEP 21

Before serving, prepare the coulis put the raspberries and sugar in the bowl of a blender and mix 1 min. You can, according to your taste, keep the small grains of the fruits in the grout, or filter it in order to have a smooth preparation. Reserve the coulis in a saucier, at room temperature. Crush the pistachios in a blender.

STEP 22

When serving, heat the honey in a small saucepan. Remove the log from the cold and remove the film. Spread honey with a brush over the entire surface of the log.

STEP 23

Spread the coconut that was used to make the milk on a board and roll the log into this nut. You can also replace it with cocoa powder, crushed pistachios, and more. Decorate with decorations made of sugar, marzipan or white chocolate

STEP 24

Cut the log into oblique slices and serve with coulis.

14. Christmas Cookies With Hazelnuts

PREPARATION GUIDE: CHRISTMAS BISCUITS WITH HAZELNUTS

- Number of persons: 6 Pers.
- Preparation time: 10 minutes
- Cooking time: 15 min
- Difficulty: Easy

INGREDIENTS

- 225 g flour

- 65 g of hazelnut powder

- 145 g of butter

- 125 g of brown sugar

- 2 egg yolks

- 1 teaspoon of cinnamon

- some hazelnuts

- 1 pinch of salt

PREPARATION

STEP 1

Preheat the oven th.5 / 6 (160 ° C).

2ND STEP

In a container, work the butter and sugar with a wooden spoon to obtain an ointment. Add the egg yolks, cinnamon, flour, hazelnut powder and salt. Mix to obtain a ball of soft dough.

STEP 3

Lightly flour the work surface, spread the dough with a roll about 1 cm thick. Cut the shortbreads with the cookie cutter. Sprinkle with hazelnuts that you have crushed roughly.

STEP 4

Arrange the cookies on the baking sheet lined with parchment paper and bake for about 15 minutes, until golden brown. Let cool on the plate.

STEP 5

Before serving, sprinkle with icing sugar or brown sugar each small Christmas cake. You can now serve your nutty dessert!

TIPS

You can revisit this Christmas dessert recipe by replacing hazelnuts with walnuts, almonds, praline or peanuts. You can decorate your little cookies with homemade icing and make drawings on them. Get creative!

15. Frozen Christmas Cookies

PREPARATION GUIDE GLAZED CHRISTMAS BISCUITS

- Number of persons: 6 Pers.
- Preparation time: 30 min

- Cooking time: 10 minutes
- Recipe cost: Cheap
- Difficulty: Easy

INGREDIENTS

For the biscuit

- 400 g of wheat flour

- 150g of sweet butter

- 2 eggs

- 100 g caster sugar

- 11 g of baking powder

- 10 pieces of green cardamom capsules

- 3 pieces of star anise

For icing

- 225 g icing sugar

- 1 egg white

- 1 cl of lemon juice

PREPARATION

STEP 1

For the biscuit

2ND STEP

Preheat the oven th.7 (200 ° C).

STEP 3

Finely chop the green cardamom capsules and star anise stars in a mortar.

STEP 4

Take a pan and put in the crushed spices and butter.

STEP 5

Cook until you get a nutty butter. Pass the mixture through a fine strainer.

STEP 6

Leave aside.

STEP 7

Assemble the baking powder and flour.

STEP 8

In a bowl, blanch the eggs and sugar.

STEP 9

Add little warm butter and flour.

STEP 10

With the fingertips, knead everything to have a smooth dough.

STEP 11

Use a rolling pin and place the rolling pin on baking paper.

STEP 12

Keep cool for 30 minutes.

STEP 13

Using a cookie cutter, detail the dough.

STEP 14

Spread the set on baking paper.

STEP 15

Bake for 10 minutes and let cool.

STEP 16

For icing

STEP 17

In a bowl, assemble the egg white and icing sugar.

STEP 18

Pour in the lemon juice.

STEP 19

Smooth the whole with a whip.

STEP 20

Let the glaze crust for 20 minutes at room temperature.

STEP 21

It's ready! You can serve cold or lukewarm frozen Christmas cookies.

16. Wolf Tooth Biscuits

PREPARATION GUIDE: BISCUITS TEETH WOLF

- Number of persons: 3 Pers.
- Preparation time: 15 min
- Difficulty: Easy

INGREDIENTS

- 350 g flour

- 200 g caster sugar

- 250 g of soft butter

- 3 whole eggs

- 1 sheet saw tooth

PREPARATION

STEP 1

Preheat the oven to 180 ° C.

2ND STEP

Whisk the whole eggs in a salad bowl.

STEP 3

Add the flour, caster sugar and soft butter and beat again until smooth and creamy.

STEP 4

Grease with a knob of butter the saw tooth.

STEP 5

Pour 2 small pieces of dough into the hollow parts of the saw tooth plate.

STEP 6

Bake the sheet and cook for 15 minutes, until the dough is elongated and pointed biscuits and they are well gilded.

STEP 7

At the end of cooking, take the sheet out of the oven and let the biscuits cool on a wire rack.

STEP 8

When the cookies have cooled, peel them off the sheet with the blade of a knife.

STEP 9

Place the saw tooth biscuits in an airtight box until tasting.

STEP 10

Enjoy biscuits with a dessert cream, a sweet mousse or an ice cream.

17. Spoon Cookies Truffle With Chocolate

PREPARATION GUIDE: CHOCOLATE TRUFFLE SPOON BISCUITS

- Number of persons: 8 Pers.
- Preparation time: 50 min
- Cooking time: 18 min
- Rest time: 2 h 10 min
- Difficulty: Easy

INGREDIENTS

For cookies:

- 125 g caster sugar

- 60 g of flour

- 60 g of potato starch

- 30 g icing sugar

- 5 whole eggs

For truffles:

- 300 g dark chocolate

- 125 g icing sugar

- 100 g of butter

- 5 cl thick cream

- 2 egg yolks

- 1 tablespoon of milk

- Bitter cocoa powder

PREPARATION

STEP 1

Prepare the cookies:

2ND STEP

Preheat the oven th.6 (180 ° C).

STEP 3

Mix the flour and starch together.

STEP 4

Separate the egg whites and yolks, reserve the whites.

STEP 5

In a large bowl, whisk together the yolks and half of the caster sugar until the mixture is white.

STEP 6

Using a robot, mount the whites to snow. When they turn white and sparkling, add the other half of the caster sugar and continue whisking until they are firm.

STEP 7

Gently add the sugar-yellow mixture of eggs to the egg whites.

STEP 8

Mix lightly and slowly stir in the flour-starch mixture. You must obtain a smooth and homogeneous mixture.

STEP 9

On a baking sheet covered with parchment paper, shape cookies using a pastry bag.

STEP 10

Sprinkle your cookies with icing sugar. Wait 10 minutes then repeat and bake immediately.

STEP 11

Bake for about 15 minutes until you get a nice color.

STEP 12

Take out of the oven and let cool.

STEP 13

Prepare the truffles:

STEP 14

Melt the chocolate in a Bain Marie. Pour the milk and mix until the chocolate is melted.

STEP 15

Gradually add the butter cubes, then the egg yolks one by one, the thick cream and the icing sugar. Whisk the dough for 5 min.

STEP 16

Pour your mixture into a cake tin and put it in the fridge for 2 hours.

STEP 17

Pour the bitter cocoa into a plate, take the dough out of the fridge.

STEP 18

Using a small spoon, take small amounts of dough and quickly form balls between your fingers. Ride immediately in the cocoa.

STEP 19

Once your truffles are done, arrange them on your biscuits with a spoon and serve!

TIPS

Perfect to accompany coffee!

18. Christmas Cookies With Spices

PREPARATION GUIDE CHRISTMAS BISCUITS WITH SPICES

- Number of persons: 8 Pers.
- Preparation time: 20 min
- Cooking time: 10 minutes
- Recipe cost: Cheap
- Difficulty: Easy

INGREDIENTS

- 250g of flour

- 1 egg

- 1 teaspoon baking powder

- 1 teaspoon of 4 spices

- 100 grams of butter

- 125 grams of honey

- 100 grams of brown sugar

- Egg white

- Icing sugar

PREPARATION

STEP 1

Mix the flour, yeast and spices in a bowl.

2ND STEP

Melt the butter in a bain-marie. Let cool and add honey, powdered sugar and beaten eggs. Mix.

STEP 3

Gradually add the flour and spices mixture and knead the dough to obtain a fairly compact consistency. If necessary, add a little flour.

STEP 4

Spread the dough on a floured work surface and cut out biscuits using a cookie cutter of the shape of your choice. Place on a baking sheet lined with baking paper. Cook for 7 to 10 minutes (oven preheated to 180 ° C). The cookies must be golden brown.

STEP 5

Cool the cookies. Using a pastry pen, decorate the shortbreads with a mixture of icing sugar and egg white. Dry the icing before tasting the cookies.

19. Chilled Strawberry, Vanilla And Chocolate Log

PREPARATION GUIDE STRAWBERRY ICE, VANILLA AND CHOCOLATE LOG

- Number of persons: 6 Pers.
- Preparation time: 10 minutes
- Rest time: 3 h
- Difficulty: Easy

INGREDIENTS

- 60 cl strawberry ice cream

- 60 cl vanilla ice cream

- 60 cl of chocolate ice cream

- 2nd recipe

- 250 g of boudoirs (roses if possible)
- 250 g frozen strawberries including 12 cut in 2
- 2 big eggs
- 20 cl of liquid cream
- 1 sheet of gelatin
- 100 g melted half-salted butter
- 30 g caster sugar
- 80 g of brown sugar
- 1 pinch of salt

PREPARATION

STEP 1

Line a cake tin with food film. Spread the strawberry ice cream with a spatula. Add the vanilla ice cream and finish with the chocolate ice cream. Reserve in the freezer for at least 3 hours. Unmold with the help of the food film and serve immediately.

2ND STEP

2nd recipe

STEP 3

Line a cake tin with food film by passing the film on the sides.

STEP 4

Mix the boudoirs. Mix them in a salad bowl with the melted butter and sugar to obtain a granular paste.

STEP 5

Put half of this dough in the cake pan. Place the mold for 30 minutes in the freezer.

STEP 6

Meanwhile, soak the gelatin for 10 minutes in a bowl of cold water.

STEP 7

Mix the strawberries. Separate the egg whites from the yolks. Beat the egg whites with a pinch of salt. Beat the whipped cream in another bowl.

STEP 8

In a salad bowl, beat the yolks and the brown sugar. Add the strawberry puree.

STEP 9

Melt the drained gelatin in a saucepan with 5 cl of water and mix it with the mixture. Gently add whipped cream then whites to snow.

STEP 10

Pour the mixture into the mold, add the cut strawberries and put another 30 min in the freezer.

STEP 11

Spread the rest of the dough on top. Shoot. Allow 4 hours in the freezer.

STEP 12

Unmold the frozen strawberry, vanilla and chocolate log on a presentation dish by gently pulling the cling film.

20. Nougatine Ice Cream Log

PREPARATION GUIDE OAK GLACED OAK

- Number of persons: 6 Pers.
- Preparation time: 20 min
- Cooking time: 10 minutes
- Recipe cost: Cheap
- Difficulty: Easy

INGREDIENTS

For the biscuit

- 4 eggs

- 120 g of flour

- 125 g caster sugar

- 2 teaspoon cocoa powder

For garnish

- 3 egg whites

- 150 g of sugar

- 50 ml of water

- 200 g of very soft butter

- Marsala (sweet wine)

For the ganache

- 200 g of NOUGATINE

- 100 g of white chocolate

- 100 ml whole liquid cream

PREPARATION

STEP 1

Preheat the oven to 6. (180 ° C).

2ND STEP

Prepare the biscuit Separate the whites from the egg yolks. Beat the egg whites firmly with a pinch of salt and stir in the sugar while whisking. Beat the egg yolks with a fork and add them to the whites by gently mixing. Stir in flour and bitter cocoa powder, mixing gently.

STEP 3

Spread the mixture evenly on a baking sheet lined with parchment paper. Bake for 10 minutes. Cool on leaving the oven.

STEP 4

Peel the sponge cake and place it on another sheet of baking paper. Book.

STEP 5

Prepare the chocolate ganache Melt the chocolate cut into pieces in a bain-marie. Let cool. Assemble the liquid cream in firm Chantilly with an electric mixer. Carefully stir in the melted chocolate with a spatula. Keep cool until use.

STEP 6

Prepare the mousse Heat the sugar and water in a saucepan until you get a syrup. Beat the egg whites firmly with an electric mixer. Add the syrup while whisking until you get a smooth, shiny meringue. Add the butter ointment, stirring constantly until you get a very homogeneous butter cream.

STEP 7

For assembly soak the biscuit with a little Marsala then cover with the butter cream leaving 1 cm at the edge. Roll the biscuit and cut the ends to obtain sharp edges. Place the ganache in a pastry bag and decorate the log.

STEP 8

Break the NOUGATINE and sprinkle it on the ganache. Reserve the log in the freezer until the service.

STEP 9

Take out the log 15 minutes before tasting.

21. Chilled Cookie Log

PREPARATION GUIDE COOKIE GLAZED LOG

- Number of persons: 8 Pers.
- Preparation time: 35 min
- Recipe cost: Cheap
- Difficulty: Easy

INGREDIENTS

For the log

- 200 g of cookies

- 300 g of mascarpone

- 100 g of hard nougat

- 40 g of small meringues

- 10 cl of liquid cream

- 2 egg yolks

- 50 g brown sugar

- 50 g of butter

For the decoration

- 100 g of milk chocolate

- 200 ml whole liquid cream

- dark chocolate sauce

- black chocolate chips

PREPARATION

STEP 1

Prepare the ganache and whipped cream for decoration

2ND STEP

Add 100 ml whipped liquid whipped cream using an electric mixer.

STEP 3

Reserve the whipped cream until you use it.

STEP 4

Melt the milk chocolate cut into pieces in a bain-marie.

STEP 5

Put the remaining liquid cream in whipped cream.

STEP 6

Add the melted milk chocolate gently.

STEP 7

Book fresh until used.

STEP 8

Prepare the log

STEP 9

Whisk 2 egg yolks in a bain-marie pan with the sugar until you have a homogeneous foam.

STEP 10

Out of the heat, add the mascarpone and mix carefully.

STEP 11

Assemble the liquid cream in firm Chantilly with an electric mixer.

STEP 12

Mix the two preparations carefully with a spatula.

STEP 13

Cut into small pieces the nougat and the meringues.

STEP 14

Crush the cookies in a salad bowl. Add 1 c. sugar and melted butter, stirring well.

STEP 15

Line a cake tin with food film, leaving it overflowing, then with parchment paper.

STEP 16

Put half of the cream in the bottom of the mold and cover with the cookies and the remaining cream.

STEP 17

Fold the parchment paper and plastic film into the mold and place in the freezer at least 3 hours before tasting.

STEP 18

Fifteen minutes before serving, take out the log and turn it into a serving dish.

STEP 19

Place whipped cream and ganache in two piping bags and decorate the log to your liking.

STEP 20

Pour on the ganache and whipped cream a little chocolate sauce, using a pastry pistol.

STEP 21

Sprinkle with chocolate chips.

STEP 22

Serve immediately.

22. Ice-Cream Log With Raspberry

PREPARATION GUIDE GLAZED LOGO REVISITED WITH RASPBERRY

- Number of persons: 8 Pers.
- Preparation time: 1 h 30 min
- Cooking time: 15 min
- Difficulty: Intermediate

INGREDIENTS

For the Genoese

- 4 eggs

- 120 g caster sugar

- 120 g of flour

- 12 jar of raspberry jam

For the Bavarian raspberry

- 380 g raspberries

- 14 g of edible gelatin (7 sheets of 2g)

- 5 egg yolks

- 100 g caster sugar

- 50 cl of milk

- 30 cl of fresh cream

- 40 g icing sugar

- 1/2 teaspoon powdered vanilla

PREPARATION

STEP 1

Prepare the sponge cake

2ND STEP

Preheat oven Th.6 (180 ° C).

STEP 3

Whip a whole egg and 2 yolks with the sugar and stir in the flour.

STEP 4

Mount the 2 egg whites in snow. Add them gently to the preparation.

STEP 5

Cover a baking sheet with parchment paper and spread your preparation on it.

STEP 6

Cook for 10 minutes.

STEP 7

At the end of the oven, unmold the biscuit.

STEP 8

Spread it over the whole surface with raspberry jam.

STEP 9

Roll the biscuit tightly.

STEP 10

Put it on a dish and let it rest in the refrigerator.

STEP 11

Prepare the Bavarian

STEP 12

Mix the raspberries to obtain a coulis.

STEP 13

Soak the gelatin sheets in cold water.

STEP 14

In a bowl whit your young eggs with sugar.

STEP 15

In a saucepan, bring the milk to a boil, then remove from the heat and pour over the egg yolks.

STEP 16

Cook over low heat, stirring. When the cream laps the wooden spoon you can remove it from the fire.

STEP 17

Add the raspberry coulis and mix well.

STEP 18

Book fresh.

STEP 19

In a cold salad bowl whip the crème fraiche with the icing sugar and the vanilla.

STEP 20

Carefully add the whipped cream to the raspberry custard.

STEP 21

Add fresh raspberries to the Bavarian mousse.

STEP 22

Climb the royal charlotte

STEP 23

Cut the rolled cake into thin slices.

STEP 24

Cover a salad bowl with plastic wrap and line it with pieces of rolled biscuits, tightening them well so that there is no space between the cut slices.

STEP 25

For the Bavarian with raspberry.

STEP 26

Cover with plastic wrap on top and refrigerate for 1 night.

STEP 27

When serving, unmold your cake on a plate and gently remove the food films.

23. Light Log With Mango

PREPARATION GUIDE LIGHT MANGO LOG

- Number of persons: 6 Pers.
- Preparation time: 30 min
- Cooking time: 10 minutes
- Difficulty: Easy

INGREDIENTS

For the biscuit

- 130 g of flour

- 130 g of sugar

- 5 eggs

- For the device

- 8 mangoes

- 3 sheets of gelatin

- 50 g of sugar (aspartame)

PREPARATION

STEP 1

Preheat the oven the 6 (180 ° C).

2ND STEP

Preparation of rolled biscuit Separate the whites from the yolks. In a bowl mix yolks, sugar and flour. In another bowl, with an electric mixer, at a fast speed, whip the whites until they become firm. Using a spoon, place the whites in the previous preparation and stir gently. Pour the mixture on a rectangular plate covered with baking paper. Cook for 10 minutes. Once cooked, let the biscuit rest and roll it on itself. Place it on a dish.

STEP 3

Preparation of the mango cream Cut 7 mangoes into small cubes and mix them to make a coulis. Heat the coulis to eat the sugar in a saucepan. Cut the mango remaining in pieces for decoration. Book. Put the gelatin sheets in cold water. Add the gelatin and dilute them in the mixture. Place the fruit cooler to harden.

STEP 4

Preparing the Christmas log Spread the mango cream on the biscuit and roll it again. Decorate with powdered coconut and mango pieces. Then enjoy your exotic Christmas cake.

TIPS

You can of course decline this mango log recipe with other exotic fruits, such as pomegranate or pineapple. The apparatus is the name given to the mixture of various ingredients, used to prepare a culinary preparation, to make a dish; we also say a mass. This term is often used in pastry.

24. Light Chocolate Log

PREPARATION GUIDE LIGHT CHOCOLATE LOG

- Number of persons: 8 Pers.

- Preparation time: 30 min

- Cooking time: 10 minutes

- Rest: 1 h

- Difficulty: Easy

INGREDIENTS

For the biscuit

- 125 g of sugar

- 125 g flour

- 5 eggs

For the light chocolate device

- 250 g dark chocolate with 70% cocoa

- 250 g of 3% fat cream

PREPARATION

STEP 1

Preheat the oven the 6 (180 ° C).

2ND STEP

Preparation of the biscuit in salad bowls, separate the egg whites from the egg yolks. Whisk the whites with an electric mixer at high speed. In another bowl, mix yolks, sugar and flour. Stir in the whites gently and three times while mixing. Pour the light chocolate cookie biscuit mixture onto a baking sheet covered with baking paper. Bake on a rack at half height. Cook the biscuit for 10 min.

STEP 3

Prepare a cake tin in which you apply a sheet of baking paper or cling film. Overflow the edges. Once cooked, roll the cookie on itself and place it on a dish or in the cake pan that you have just prepared.

STEP 4

Preparing the device this is a preparation of a chocolate ganache. Boil the cream. Out of the fire add the chocolate in pieces and mix. The device must be smooth.

STEP 5

For the dressage unroll the biscuit, spread half of the ganache and roll it. Arrange the other part of the ganache on the biscuit and reserve 2 hours in the refrigerator.

STEP 6

Unmold the light chocolate log and place on a platter. Decorate it.

TIPS

The apparatus is the name given to the mixture of various ingredients, used to prepare a culinary preparation, to make a dish; we also say a mass. This term is often used in pastry.

25. Raspberry Mousse Log

PREPARATION GUIDE FRAMBOISE MOUSSE FOAM

- Number of persons: 8 Pers.
- Preparation time: 25 min
- Cooking time: 12 min
- Recipe cost: Cheap
- Difficulty: Easy

INGREDIENTS

For the biscuit

- 100g of flour

- 4 eggs

- 30 g bitter cocoa powder

- 90 g of sugar

For raspberry mousse

- 100 g fresh or thawed raspberries

- 200 g of liquid cream

- 30 g of sugar

- 3 sheets of gelatin

For raspberry coulis

- 120 g fresh or thawed raspberries

PREPARATION

STEP 1

Prepare the raspberry coulis Heat the raspberries with a little water in a saucepan, until you get a compote. Mix the compote in a blender until grout. Let the grout cool.

2ND STEP

Prepare the raspberry mousse

STEP 3

Soften the gelatin sheets in a bowl of cold water. Mix the raspberries with the sugar in a blender until you get a puree. Pass the puree to the Chinese. Pour the raspberry purée into a saucepan and heat to a low heat. Add the wrung gelatin off the heat and mix well. Let cool. Beat the whipped cream in a bowl and add the raspberry puree. Mix gently. Reserve the raspberry mousse in the refrigerator.

STEP 4

Prepare the biscuit

STEP 5

Preheat the oven to 180 ° C. Separate the egg whites from the yolks. Beat the eggs with the sugar in a salad bowl. Add the flour and cocoa and mix. Beat the egg whites firmly with an electric mixer. Add them gently to the previous mixture. Spread the dough on a rectangular baking sheet covered with baking paper. Bake for 12 minutes. Unmold the biscuit on a damp cloth at the exit of the oven. Roll it on itself immediately and allow it to cool.

STEP 6

Mounting

STEP 7

Unroll the biscuit and coat the surface with raspberry coulis. Spread raspberry mousse on top with a spatula. Roll the biscuit on itself, lengthwise, then cut the ends.

TIPS

You can decorate your log with chocolate ganache all around to form a real log!

26. Log Walnuts Strudel Way

PREPARATION GUIDE LOG LOGS APPLES NUTS WAY STRUDEL

- Number of persons: 6 Pers.
- Preparation time: 25 min
- Cooking time: 30 min
- Difficulty: Easy

INGREDIENTS

- 60 g of butter

- 4 tablespoons caster sugar

- 2 Golden apples

- 2 bags of vanilla sugar

- 3 tablespoons walnut powder

- ½ teaspoon of cinnamon powder

- 50 g icing sugar

- 6 sheets of brick

- 10 nuts

PREPARATION

STEP 1

Preheat your oven to th.6 (180 ° C).

2ND STEP

Peel, seed and cut apples into thin slices.

STEP 3

In a bowl, mix together the powdered sugar and the vanilla sugar.

STEP 4

Melt the butter and, using a brush, spread it on a sheet of brick. Sprinkle 1 tablespoon of the mixture of the two sugars on the buttered brick sheet. Put a second sheet of pastry on top and repeat the operation butter, sugar and pastry sheet until you have superimposed the 6 sheets of brick on top of each other.

STEP 5

Add the cinnamon to the mixture of two remaining sugars. Butter the last pastry sheet and sprinkle half of the sugar and cinnamon mixture.

STEP 6

Crush the nuts. Put the apple slices and the crushed nuts on the pastry sheets, sprinkle again with the mixture of sugars and cinnamon.

STEP 7

Wrap the stacked leaflets on themselves by tucking the ends inside to enclose the apple and walnut filling.

STEP 8

Line the baking sheet of your oven with parchment paper. Put your log walnuts with strudel on the plate, brush it with the remaining melted butter. Bake for 30 minutes.

STEP 9

Let cool before sprinkling the icing sugar on your strudel apple-walnut log to decorate it.

TIPS

Follow your strudel-style apple-walnut log with a delicious whipped cream for an even greedy dessert.

27. Brownie With Walnut Kernels

PREPARATION GUIDE BROWNIE WITH NUTS

- Number of persons: 4 Pers.
- Preparation time: 15 min
- Cooking time: 20 min
- Difficulty: Easy

INGREDIENTS

- 125 g of chocolate

- 200 g of sugar

- 4 eggs

- 200 g dark chocolate dessert

- 2 tablespoons flour

- 100 g walnuts

PREPARATION

STEP 1

Preheat the oven to th.7 (200 ° C).

2ND STEP

Melt the chocolate with the butter in a saucepan.

STEP 3

Meanwhile, mix in a bowl the sugar, the flour and the eggs.

STEP 4

Add the melted chocolate. Mix well and add the crushed walnut kernels. Mix.

STEP 5

Pour into a square pan and bake for about 20 minutes.

STEP 6

Serve warm and cut into pieces.

28. Vanilla Brownie

PREPARATION GUIDE BROWNIE VANILLÉ

- Number of persons: 4 Pers.
- Preparation time: 20 min
- Cooking time: 20 min
- Difficulty: Easy

INGREDIENTS

- 125 g of butter

- 75 g of chocolate to cook

- 200 g of sugar

- 2 eggs

- 75 g flour

- a few drops of liquid vanilla extract

- 75 g shelled walnuts

- icing sugar

- 3 striped barley sugars

PREPARATION

STEP 1

Preheat your oven th.5 (150 ° C).

2ND STEP

Melt the chocolate and butter together, over low heat or in a bain-marie, stirring gently with a wooden spoon. Avoid boiling which would give a grainy chocolate look.

STEP 3

Out of the heat, add the sugar by mixing quickly. You have to get a smooth and shiny dough.

STEP 4

Stir in the eggs one by one, beating the mixture with a fork.

STEP 5

Add the flour in small doses, stirring briskly, then the nuts and vanilla. Mix everything well.

STEP 6

Butter a rectangular mold about 20 cm by 24 cm and pour the dough into it.

STEP 7

Crush the barley sugars and sprinkle them on the brownie, then bake for 20 min.

29. Cheesecake With Cookies

PREPARATION GUIDE CHEESECAKE COOKIES

- Number of persons: 7 Pers.
- Preparation time: 30 min
- Cooking time: 1 h
- Rest: 12 h
- Difficulty: Easy

INGREDIENTS

- 130 g softened butter

- 150 g caster sugar

- 80 g flour

- 4 eggs

- 20 cl of fresh cream

- 1 tablespoon icing sugar

- 1 untreated lemon

- 1 sachet of vanilla sugar

- 500 g cottage cheese

- 300 g of cookies

- a pinch of nutmeg

- a pinch of fine salt

PREPARATION

STEP 1

The day before

2ND STEP

Let the cheese drizzle in the refrigerator for at least 12 hours.

STEP 3

The same day

STEP 4

Preheat your oven the 6 (180 ° C).

STEP 5

Take the zest of the lemon and blanch it for 5 minutes in boiling water. Rinse it, dry it, and then detail it in fine julienne.

STEP 6

Squeeze the lemon and preserve its juice.

STEP 7

Crush cookies with a rolling pin or crumble them by hand. Blend this breadcrumbs with 100 g softened butter. Add the salt.

STEP 8

Butter a pie dish 27 cm in diameter with the remaining butter, then spread the dough of cookies with your fingers.

STEP 9

Pour the liquid cream into a salad bowl and let it cool for a few minutes in the freezer.

STEP 10

In a bowl, whip the cottage cheese until it is smooth. While continuing to beat, add the caster sugar, the vanilla sugar, the pinch of freshly grated nutmeg, and the egg yolks one by one, the flour in rain, the zest and the juice of the lemon.

STEP 11

Take the cream out of the freezer and whip it in whipped cream. When it is very firm and forms crests, mix it delicately with the beaten white cheese.

STEP 12

Beat the egg whites until stiff, adding the icing sugar at the end. Stir in the pending mixture.

STEP 13

Pour this dish over the cookie dough, smooth the surface and bake halfway up. Cook for 1 hour. Then leave another 15 minutes in the oven, leaving the door open.

STEP 14

Let cool completely before turning out carefully with two dishes turn the pan on a dish (the cake is upside down), then turn the cheesecake on another dish to put it back to the place!

TIPS

It is important that the cottage cheese is well drained. We can replace the 80 g of flour by 2 tablespoons of corn flour.

30. Biscuits With Orange

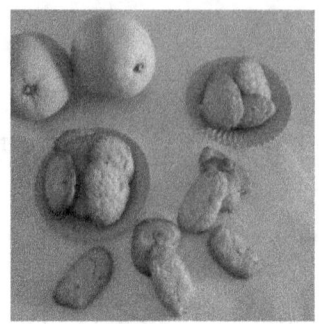

PREPARATION GUIDE ORANGE FINE BISCUITS

- Number of persons: 8 Pers.
- Preparation time: 15 min
- Cooking time: 20 min
- Rest: 1 h
- Recipe cost: Cheap
- Difficulty: Easy

INGREDIENTS

- 200 grams of flour

- 1 sachet of baking powder

- 1 sachet of vanilla sugar

- 120 grams of soft butter

- the juice and zest of an orange

- 60 grams of corn flour

- 100 grams of powdered sugar

- 1 egg

PREPARATION

STEP 1

Mix the flour, baking powder and cornstarch.

2ND STEP

Then add the sugars, egg and diced butter. Knead the dough and finish by incorporating the zest and the orange juice.

STEP 3

Place the dough in plastic film and roll into the shape of a rectangular pudding. Put in the refrigerator for a minimum hour.

STEP 4

After the rest time, cut out slices of dough (about ½ cm thick) and place them on a plate covered with baking paper.

STEP 5

Bake for 20 minutes (oven preheated to 180 ° C). The biscuits should be lightly browned.

31. Cornets Of Beggar Pancakes

PREPARATION GUIDE MEN'S CREPPERS CORNETS

- Number of persons: 4 Pers.
- Preparation time: 30 min
- Cooking time: 10 minutes
- Difficulty: Easy

INGREDIENTS

- 4 pancakes

- 300 g candied fruit

- 2 tablespoons rum

- 75 g slivered almonds

-For custard

- 1 l of milk

- 1 vanilla pod

- 6 eggs

- 150 g of sugar

PREPARATION

STEP 1

Prepare the cream

2ND STEP

Boil the milk with the vanilla bean split lengthwise. When boiling, turn off the heat and let it steep.

STEP 3

Meanwhile, whisk the egg yolks with the sugar until the mixture whitens.

STEP 4

Add, without stopping whipping, the hot milk without the vanilla pod. Put the mixture back in the pan and thicken over low heat, turning always.

STEP 5

Let cool and reserve in the fridge at least an hour before serving.

STEP 6

Prepare the pancakes

STEP 7

Warm up the pancakes. Detail the diced candied fruit and soak in the rum. Grill the almonds.

STEP 8

Garnish the pancakes with the candied fruit mixture, sprinkle 34 of the almonds. Fold the pancakes into a cone, sprinkle with the remaining almonds and serve with custard.

32. Cream Cheese And Cream Of Chestnut

PREPARATION GUIDE EXPRESS WHITE CHEESE CREAM AND BROWN CREAM

- Number of persons: 2 Pers.
- Preparation time: 8 min
- Cooking time: 1 h
- Difficulty: Easy

INGREDIENTS

- 150 g of white cheese

- 80 g of brown cream

- 1 pinch of vanilla powder

- 70 g of flaked almonds (optional)

PREPARATION

STEP 1

In a salad bowl, mix the cream of brown and cottage cheese.

2ND STEP

Add the vanilla and mix.

STEP 3

Fill the cups with the mixture, then reserve in the refrigerator for at least 1 hour.

STEP 4

Sprinkle with flaked almonds when serving.

33. Homemade Apple Crumble And Homemade Chestnut Cream

PREPARATION GUIDE APPLE CRUMBLE AND HOME BROWN CREAM

- Number of persons: 4 Pers.
- Preparation time: 15 min
- Cooking time: 30 min
- Difficulty: Easy

INGREDIENTS

- 3 apples

- 9 biscuits

- 12 lemon

- 15 g of brown cream

- 1 sachet of vanilla sugar

- 60 g brown sugar

- 30 g of flour

- 80 g of butter

PREPARATION

STEP 1

Preheat the oven th.6-7 (200 ° C).

2ND STEP

Squeeze the half lemon. Peel, seed and dice the apples.

STEP 3

Spread them in an oven pan and sprinkle with lemon juice.

STEP 4

Divide the brown cream over, then sprinkle with vanilla sugar.

STEP 5

In a salad bowl, crumble the biscuits, add the flour and the brown sugar. Mix.

STEP 6

Stir in the butter and knead to a sandy mixture. Pour this mixture on apples and chestnut cream, then bake for 30 minutes.

STEP 7

Serve.

34. Fondant With Chocolate And Brown Cream

PREPARATION GUIDE: CHOCOLATE FOUNDATION AND BROWN CREAM

- Number of persons: 8 Pers.
- Preparation time: 15 min
- Cooking time: 35 min
- Difficulty Easy

INGREDIENTS

- 500 g of brown cream

- 3 eggs

- 3 tablespoons flour

- 100 g of chocolate

- 100 g of butter

- icing sugar

PREPARATION

STEP 1

Preheat the oven to 180 ° C (th.6).

2ND STEP

Break the chocolate into pieces and melt it in a bain-marie with the butter. Mix thoroughly to obtain a homogeneous cream.

STEP 3

Remove from heat and pour into a salad bowl, then add the brown cream.

STEP 4

Mix well, and add the eggs one by one, whisking.

STEP 5

Sift the flour over the bowl. Mix to obtain a homogeneous paste.

STEP 6

Divide the mixture into a silicone mold and bake for 35 minutes.

STEP 7

Unmold the fondant at the end of cooking, place it on a dish and sprinkle with icing sugar. Serve with custard.

35. Chocolate Cake With Raspberry

PREPARATION GUIDE CHOCOLATE AND RASPBERRY CAKE

- Number of persons: 8 pers.
- Preparation time: 30 min
- Cooking time: 40 min
- Rest: 3 h
- Difficulty: Easy

INGREDIENTS

- 125 g flour

- 200 g dark chocolate

- 200 g frozen raspberries

- 4 eggs

- 100 g of butter

- 70 g of sugar

- 1 packet of baking powder

-For the frosting

- 150g of sweet butter

- 150 g of dark chocolate

- 150 g icing sugar

- 1 pack of (PETIT BEURRE) or any other biscuit as in the picture.

PREPARATION

STEP 1

Preheat the oven to 180 ° C (item 6).

2ND STEP

Break the chocolate into pieces in a bowl. Add the butter and melt it in a bain-marie.

STEP 3

Break the eggs by separating the yolks from the egg whites.

STEP 4

Add the sugar to the yolks and whip until blanching. Stir in melted chocolate mixture, mix.

STEP 5

Spread the flour and half of the yeast packet through the sieve and add them, then mix again.

STEP 6

Beat the egg whites into firm snow and gently add to the mixture. Pour half of the mixture into a buttered mold.

STEP 7

Sprinkle half of the raspberries, cover with the other half of dough and bake for 40 minutes. Let cool on a rack.

STEP 8

In a saucepan, mix chocolate and butter into pieces for icing. When they are melted, add the icing sugar off the heat. Let cool.

STEP 9

Once the cake has cooled, cover it with the frosting. Immediately glue the Small Butter on the sides of the cake to cover them.

STEP 10

Decorate with the remaining raspberries and place in the refrigerator for 3 hours.

STEP 11

Serve.

36. Dark Chocolate Crepe Cake

PREPARATION GUIDE BLACK CHOCOLATE CRÊPES CAKE

- Number of persons: 4 Pers.
- Preparation time: 30 min
- Cooking time: 10 minutes
- Rest: 3 h
- Difficulty: Easy

INGREDIENTS

- 150 g of flour

- 3 eggs

- 40 cl of milk

- 1 tablespoon of brown sugar or sugar

- a tear of Grand Marnier or vanilla

- 60 g half-salted butter

- salt

- ganache

- 200 g dark chocolate

- 200 g of fresh cream

PREPARATION

STEP 1

Prepare the pancakes by mixing the flour, eggs, brown sugar and salt.

2ND STEP

Mix with the milk and mix well.

STEP 3

Add 40 g melted but cooled butter to prevent pancakes from sticking. Stir in the fragrance (Grand Marnier or vanilla).

STEP 4

Prepare the ganache by heating the cream over very low heat. Melt the chocolate. Cook a dozen pancakes. If you have a nonstick pan you do not need butter.

STEP 5

Divide the ganache in half and beat in one. Arrange the pancakes in a buttered baking pan that is slightly smaller than the pancakes.

STEP 6

Place a pancake and spread the uncooked ganache, repeat until half of the pancakes and spread a very thick layer of ganache beaten.

STEP 7

Cover with the last pancakes spread (except the last one).

STEP 8

Rest for 3 hours in the refrigerator.

STEP 9

Serve with whipped cream or vanilla flavored custard.

37. Christmas Cake (Christmas Cake)

PREPARATION GUIDE ENGLISH CHRISTMAS CAKE (CHRISTMAS CAKE)

- Number of persons: 6 Pers.
- Preparation time: 40 min
- Cooking time: 2 h 30 min
- Difficulty: Easy

INGREDIENTS

-For the cake

- 250g of flour

- 250 g of butter

- 250 g caster sugar

- 4 eggs

- 400 g of currants

- 100 g candied orange peel

- 50 g candied cherries

- 50 g slivered almonds

- 3 tablespoons cognac

- 1 teaspoon of mixture 4 spices

- 1 tablespoon of honey

-For the frosting

- 1 kg sifted icing sugar

- 1 lemon

- 4 egg whites

PREPARATION

STEP 1

Preheat the oven to the 3 4 (70 ° C).

2ND STEP

Preparation of the cake

STEP 3

In a bowl, mix the softened butter and sugar. Add 4 eggs, one by one, while stirring.

STEP 4

In another container, pour the flour. Add currants, honey, candied oranges and cherries, flaked almonds, 4 spice mixture and mix.

STEP 5

Add this preparation to the salad bowl containing the butter-sugar mixture. Mix again.

STEP 6

Butter a mold 20 cm in diameter.

STEP 7

Line it with a double layer of parchment paper, letting the paper cover about 4 cm outside.

STEP 8

Spread the dough in the mold and bake for 2 h 30, then let cool.

STEP 9

Preparation of the icing

STEP 10

Squeeze the lemon juice.

STEP 11

Beat the egg whites until smooth, then gently stir in the lemon juice and icing sugar until smooth.

STEP 12

Cover the cake over its entire surface. Equalize with a wet spatula.

STEP 13

Draw patterns on the cake, if you wish, using a pocket with a fluted socket.

STEP 14

Let dry, then store the cake in an airtight box for ten days.

38. Lemon And Yogurt Ice Cream

PREPARATION GUIDE LEMON ICE AND YOGURTS

- Number of persons: 4 Pers.
- Preparation time: 20 min
- Cooking time: 3 h
- Difficulty: Easy

INGREDIENTS

- 2 untreated lemons

- 4 natural yogurts

- 2 egg whites

- powdered sweetener

- 1 pinch of salt

- 4 barley striped Christmas sugars

PREPARATION

STEP 1

Brush lemons under hot water. Wipe them and then finely grate the zests and squeeze their juice.

2ND STEP

Pour the yogurts in a bowl. Add the juice of the lemons and grated zest. Sugar at your convenience with the powdered sweetener.

STEP 3

Mix for about 3 minutes with a low-speed electric whisk.

STEP 4

Beat the egg whites firmly with the pinch of salt and stir in the previous mixture, stirring briskly, without fear of dropping them.

STEP 5

Take in an ice cream maker.

STEP 6

Present the ice in glasses or cups, sprinkled with crushed barley sugars.

TIPS

Prefer unsweetened whole yoghurts to yoghurts. They are slightly more caloric but more creamy and tasty.

39. Layer Cake With Macaroons

PREPARATION GUIDE LAYER CAKE WITH MACARONS

- Number of persons: 8 Pers.
- Preparation time: 30 min
- Cooking time: 15 min
- Recipe cost: Cheap
- Difficulty: Easy

INGREDIENTS

For the cake

- 400 g flour

- 400 g of sugar

- 300 g of soft butter

- 30 cl of whole milk

- 5 eggs

- 1 teaspoon of natural vanilla flavor

- 2 bags of baking powder

For whipped cream

- 500 g of mascarpone

- 300 g Philadelphia cheese

- 2 lemons

- 175 g icing sugar

-For the decoration

- 6 macaroons (perfumes and colors of your choice)

PREPARATION

STEP 1

Prepare the cake. Preheat your oven to 180 ° C. Beat the eggs with the sugar in a salad bowl. Add the soft butter, flour and yeast and mix vigorously.

2ND STEP

Add milk and vanilla. Mix well. Place a sheet of baking paper in the bottom of a buttered and floured circular cake pan. Cook the sponge cake one by one for 10 minutes. Let the four sponge cakes on a grill.

STEP 3

Prepare the whipped cream. Squeeze the juice of the lemons. Mix the mascarpone, the Philadelphia, the juice of the 2 lemons and the sugar in a salad bowl. Reserve at room temperature until assembly.

STEP 4

For mounting. Place a first disc of sponge cake on a serving platter.

STEP 5

Cover it with frosting. Place a second disc of sponge cake on top and a new layer of frosting. Repeat for the other two sponge discs. Cover the entire cake with the remaining frosting, smoothing the edges well.

STEP 6

Decorate the top of the Layer Cake with the macaroons. Reserve the cake in the fridge for 2 hours.

TIPS

For a beautifully colored Macaroon Layer Cake, you can add a few drops of food coloring to the cake batter. Divide the dough into 4 salad bowls. Choose a single color and add more or less drops in each bowl. Mix well to get a nice color gradient.

40. Layer Chocolate Cheesecake, Ferrero® And Nutella®

PREPARATION GUIDE CHOCOLATE, FERRERO® AND NUTELLA® CHOCOLATE CHEESECAKE LAYER

- Number of persons: 6 Pers.
- Preparation time: 45 min
- Cooking time: 1 h 30 min
- Affordable
- Difficulty: difficult

- Dark chocolate

- 8 cl of peanut oil

- -For mounting

- 12 Ferrero Roche

PREPARATION

STEP 1

For chocolate sponge cake

2ND STEP

Preheat the oven to 200 ° C (6-7).

STEP 3

Butter and flour a mold to miss. Sift together the flour and the cocoa powder.

STEP 4

In a bowl, beat the eggs with the sugar on the electric mixer until the mixture becomes foamy and triple in volume.

STEP 5

Gently stir in the flour-cocoa mixture, then pour into the mold.

STEP 6

Bake for 20 minutes, then let cool.

STEP 7

For the Nutella cheesecake

STEP 8

Preheat the oven to 160 ° C. Plan two grids in the oven, the first one down, the second one in the middle. On the bottom, bake a gratin dish filled with water it will prevent the cheesecake from drying out.

STEP 9

Melt the chocolate in a bain-marie stirring, then let it warm.

STEP 10

In a bowl, whip the Philadelphia, Nutella and vanilla until the mixture is creamy.

STEP 11

Gradually add the sugar, then the eggs one by one. Finish with the cream and melted chocolate, mixing after each addition to obtain a smooth paste.

STEP 12

Divide the mixture into a buttered pan or silicone pan of the same size as the sponge cake. Bake at half height for 40 to 50 minutes check the cooking, the cream should be taken as a custard.

STEP 13

At the end of the oven, put the cheesecake on a rack. Immediately pass a very cold spatula between the edges of the mold and the edges of the cake, to avoid cracking it while cooling. Let it cool for 1 hour, then reserve 5 hours in the refrigerator.

STEP 14

- For Ferrero ganache

STEP 15

Melt the Ferrero in a saucepan with the milk chocolate broken into pieces, over very low heat and stirring.

STEP 16

Gradually add the cream. Mix well, pour into a bowl and let cool.

STEP 17

For icing

STEP 18

Melt the chocolate in a Bain Marie. Out of the fire, add the oil and mix well.

STEP 19

For mounting

STEP 20

Cut the sponge cake in half in thickness. Cover each half of a layer of ganache with Ferrero.

STEP 21

Carefully unmount the cheesecake. Place it on a half of sponge covered with ganache, then close with the second, ganache inward.

STEP 22

Pour over the hot icing on the top of the cake, center, and let it flow naturally on the sides.

STEP 23

Place the Ferrero all around the cake, pressing lightly to fix them in the frosting. Let cool, then reserve 2 hours in the refrigerator before serving.

Part 2

Main Course

Sunday Rib Roast

Yield: 6 to 8 servings Level: Easy

- [ ] 1 (3-rib) standing rib roast (7 to 8 pounds)
- [ ] 1 tablespoon kosher salt
- [ ] 1 1/2 teaspoons freshly ground black pepper
- [ ] Mustard Horseradish Sauce, recipe follows
- [ ] 1 1/2 cups good mayonnaise
- [ ] 3 tablespoons Dijon mustard
- [ ] 1 1/2 tablespoons wholegrain mustard
- [ ] 1 tablespoon prepared horseradish
- [ ] 1/3 cup sour cream
- [ ] 1/4 teaspoon kosher salt

Christmas Recipies

directions:
- [ ] Two hours before roasting, remove the meat from the refrigerator and allow it to come to room temperature.
- [ ] Preheat the oven to 500 degrees F.
- [ ] Place the oven rack on the second lowest position.

☐ Place the roast in a pan big enough to hold it, boneside down, and spread the top thickly with the salt and pepper. Roast the meat for 45 minutes. Without removing the meat from the oven, reduce the oven temperature to 325 degrees F and roast for another 30 minutes. Finally, increase the temperature to 450 degrees F and roast for another 15 to 30 minutes, until the internal temperature of the meat is 125 degrees F, inserting the thermometer is exactly in the center of the roast. The total cooking time will be around 1 1/2 hours. Meanwhile, make the Mustard Horseradish sauce.

☐ Remove the roast from the oven and transfer it to a cutting board.
☐ Cover it tightly with aluminum foil and allow the meat to rest for 20 minutes. Carve and serve with the sauce.
☐ Mustard Horseradish Sauce: Whisk together the mayonnaise, mustards, horseradish, sour cream, and salt in a small bowl.

Breakfast Casserole

Yield:8 servings Level:Easy

- ☐ 4 slices white bread
- ☐ Butter, for greasing
- ☐ 1 pound mixed mild and medium sausage, such as Salt Lick sausage
- ☐ 2 cups half-and-half
- ☐ 1 teaspoon dry mustard
- ☐ 1/2 teaspoon salt
- ☐ Pinch of pepper
- ☐ Dash hot sauce
- ☐ 6 beaten eggs
- ☐ 8 ounces fresh mushrooms, sliced, optional
- ☐ 1 1/2 cups thinly sliced, cooked unpeeled red ptatoes
- ☐ 1 cup grated Cheddar
- ☐ 1 cup grated Monterey Jack cheese

directions:

- ☐ Cube the bread and place it in a lightly greased 8-by-11-by-2 inch casserole.
- ☐ Fry the sausage until it is browned fully and drain on some paper towels.

☐ Mix the half-and-half, dry mustard, salt, pepper, hot sauce and eggs together. Layer the sausage over the bread and top with a generous layer of potatoes. If you are using mushrooms, layer them in before the potatoes. Sprinkle the cheeses on the top. Pour the beaten egg mixture over the casserole. Cover and refrigerate 1 hour to overnight.

- ☐ Preheat the oven to 350 degrees F.
- ☐ Bake the casserole until it is set and does not jiggle in the middle, 30 minutes.

Christmas Roast Duck With Crispy Potatoes

Serves: 10 Level: Medium

a few sprigs of fresh rosemary
½ nutmeg grated
sea salt
freshly ground black pepper
2 oranges or blood oranges, zested and halved
2 x 2 kg whole ducks, necks and giblets reserved and roughly chopped
8 cloves garlic, unpeeled
3 red onions, peeled and quartered
a few stalks celery, trimmed and chopped into chunks
3 carrots, scrubbed and chopped into chunks
½ stick cinnamon
1 thumb-sized piece fresh ginger, peeled and roughly chopped
a few bay leaves
2 kg Maris Piper potatoes, peeled and cut into large chunks
1 litre water or organic chicken stock
2 tablespoons plain flour
200 ml red port

13
directions:

☐ This festive duck is loaded with tasty herbs and spices, and the delicious fat is used to flavor the potatoes and port gravy.

☐ Pick the leaves off one of the rosemary sprigs and place on a board with the nutmeg, orange zest, thyme and one tablespoon of sea salt. Chop everything together and rub the mixture all over the ducks, inside and out. Cover and leave in the fridge for a few hours or overnight to let the flavors penetrate.

☐ Preheat the oven to 180°C/350°F/gas 4 and place the shelves on the middle and bottom levels. Stuff the ducks with the remaining rosemary sprigs and orange halves, and the garlic cloves, then place them breast-side up, straight on to the bars of the middle shelf. Scatter the onion, celery and carrot in the bottom of a large, deepsided roasting tray with the cinnamon, ginger, bay leaves, and chopped duck neck and giblets. Place on the bottom shelf beneath the ducks so it will catch all the lovely fat that drips out of them.

☐ Meanwhile, place the potatoes in a pan. Cover with cold, salted water, bring to a simmer and parboil for 5 to 10 minutes, then tip into a colander and chuff them up.

☐ After the duck has roasted for an hour, take the bottom tray out of the oven, replacing it with an empty tray. Spoon the fat from the veggie tray into a bowl. Put all the vegetables, duck bits and juices into a large saucepan, then add a little boiling water to the tray to get all the sticky brown bits off the bottom – you will use it to make your gravy with. Tip the water and brown bits into the pan with the veg, top up with 1 litre of water or chicken stock and place on a medium heat, skimming off any of the fat that rises to the top.

☐ Put your parboiled potatoes into the empty tray in the oven. Add a

14 few more tablespoons of duck fat from the bowl, season, and place back underneath the ducks to cook for an hour. Christmas Recipies

☐ Put your parboiled potatoes into the empty tray in the oven. Add a few more tablespoons of duck fat from the bowl, season, and place back underneath the ducks to cook for an hour.

☐ Meanwhile, heat a saucepan and add 2 tablespoons of duck fat. When it's hot and melted, add the flour and stir with a wooden spoon until you have a paste. Stir in the contents of the saucepan and the port. Bring the gravy to the boil and simmer gently for half an hour, stirring occasionally. By now the ducks will have had 2 hours in the oven and will be done. Lift them on to a plate, cover loosely with tin foil and leave to rest for about 15 minutes.

☐ Pour the gravy through a sieve into a clean saucepan, pressing down on all the veg and other bits to extract as many flavours and juices as you can. Keep the gravy warm in the saucepan, again skimming off any fat on the surface.

☐ Don't carve the ducks- the best thing to do is to pull the meat away from the bones with a pair of tongs or with your fingers wearing clean kitchen gloves, then let everyone fight over the delicious skin! Serve with your potatoes and port gravy.

ingredients: Christmas

Whole Baked Salmon In Recipies Salt

Serves: 12 Level: Medium

- ☐ 1 x 3 kg whole salmon, gutted, gills removed, scales left on
- ☐ 4 lemons
- ☐ 2 fennel bulbs
- ☐ ½ a bunch of fresh flat leaf parsley
- ☐ ½ a bunch of fresh marjoram
- ☐ ½ a bunch of fresh chives
- ☐ 4 kg rock salt
- ☐ 2 large free-range eggs
- ☐ FOR THE BASIL MAYO:

- ☐ 1 large free-range egg yolk
- ☐ 1 teaspoon English mustard
- ☐ 500 ml extra virgin olive oil
- ☐ 1 bunch of fresh basil, leaves picked
- ☐ FOR THE CHILLI SALSA:
- ☐ 1 fresh red chilli, deseeded
- ☐ ½ a bunch of fresh mint, leaves picked
- ☐ extra virgin olive oil
- ☐ white wine vinegar
- ☐ sea salt and freshly ground black pepper

Christmas Recipies

directions: ☐ Preheat the oven to 180°C/350°F/gas 4. Wash the salmon well both inside and out, then pat dry with kitchen paper (leaving the scales on helps to keep in the moisture as it cooks). Finely slice 1 lemon and the fennel into rounds and stuff into the salmon cavity with the parsley, marjoram and chives.

☐ Mix the rock salt, eggs and 250ml of water in a large bowl, spreading one-third of the salt over a large baking, making a slight hollow in the middle to hold the salmon snugly. Lay the salmon diagonally into the tray, then spoon over the remaining salt mixture, so that it's evenly covered – you should have a layer of salt, roughly 2cm thick, all over the salmon. Place the tray in the hot oven for around 40 minutes, or until cooked through. To test if the salmon is ready, push a skewer through the salt into the thickest part of the fish – if it comes out warm after 5 seconds, it's done.

☐ Meanwhile, basil mayo. Place the egg yolk and mustard into a bowl, gradually add the extra virgin olive oil. Bash the basil leaves in a pestle and mortar, then muddle in a drizzle of extra virgin olive oil until you have a smooth paste. Push the paste through a fine sieve into the mayo, stir to combine and have a taste, adding a squeeze of lemon juice or a splash of vinegar if needed, then set aside.

☐ To make the salsa, finely chop the chilli and mint leaves, then place into a bowl with 1½ tablespoons of extra virgin olive oil and 1 teaspoon of vinegar. Add salt and pepper, then set aside.

☐ Once cooked, ad allow to cool for around 20 minutes, then with the tip of a knife, carefully slice into the salt, cutting all the way along the salmon spine.

☐ Divide up the salmon and serve with the basil mayo, chilli salsa and lemon wedges for squeezing over.

ingredients:

Vegan Mushroom, Chestnut & Cranberry Tart

Serves: 8 Level: Medium

- [ ] 230g gluten-free plain flour
- [ ] FOR THE REDCURRANT GRAVY:
- [ ] 1/2 tsp xanthan gum
- [ ] 1 tbsp walnut oil, or garlic oil
- [ ] 60g dairy-free margarine
- [ ] 1 tbsp redcurrant jelly
- [ ] 60g vegetable shortening
- [ ] 300 ml hot vegetable stock
- [ ] FOR THE FILLING:
- [ ] 1 heaped tbsp corn flour, mixed with 2 tbsp water
- [ ] 1 large onion
- [ ] FOR THE ROAST POTATOES:
- [ ] 2 cloves of garlic
- [ ] 2.5 kg floury potatoes
- [ ] 6 carrots, grated (450g)
- [ ] 8 tbsp groundnut oil, or olive oil
- [ ] 250g chestnut mushrooms
- [ ] 360g peeled chestnuts
- [ ] 2 tbsp olive oil
- [ ] 1 tsp dried thyme
- [ ] 225g soya cream cheese
- [ ] 2 tbsp garlic oil
- [ ] 250 g wild mushrooms
- [ ] 2 tbsp dried cranberries
- [ ] a small bunch of fresh flat-leaf parsley
- [ ] FOR THE REDCURRANT GRAVY: 17
- [ ] 1 tbsp walnut oil, or
- [ ] Preheat the oven and a large baking tray to 180C/gas 4. Start by making the pastry. Sift the flour and xanthan gum into a food processor, add the margarine, vegetable shortening and salt and mix until

directions:

the mixture resembles breadcrumbs.

- [ ] Add 2 tablespoons of cold water, pulsing as you go, until the mixture begins to pull together to form a dough. Tip the pastry into a large bowl and, using your fingertips, pull together into a ball. Knead lightly for about 2 minutes or until smooth and elastic.

☐ 3 Shape the pastry into a ball and place between 2 large sheets of cling film, then roll it out into a circle slightly larger than the tart tin and no thinner than 3mm. Peel off the uppermost sheet of cling film and carefully flip the pastry into a deep 23cm tart tin. Peel away the remaining cling film and gently press the pastry into the sides of the tin, filling in any cracks with pastry and patting it flat with your fingertips. Trim the edges and set aside.

☐ Next, prepare the potatoes. Peel and cut in half, quartering any large ones. Place in a pan of salted water and bring to the boil. The second the water begins to boil, time the potatoes, allowing them to cook for 4 minutes before removing from the heat and draining. Pour the oil into a large roasting tin, tip in the potatoes and a heaped teaspoon of sea salt and firmly shake to coat evenly. Set aside while you make the filling for the tart.

☐ Finely chop the onion, crush the garlic, then finely grate the carrots. Trim the stalks from the chestnut mushrooms and slice into rounds. Halve 240g of the chestnuts.
☐ Heat the olive oil, add the onions and cook gently over a low heat until softened. Add the carrots, garlic, thyme and mushrooms and fry until softened– around 10 minutes.

☐ Stir in the cream cheese and halved chestnuts and mix together gently until the cheese has softened and formed a creamy mixture. Season to taste, spoon the filling into the pastry case then level the top. Place the tart on the baking tray on the top shelf of the oven and the potatoes on the bottom shelf. Bake for 35–40 minutes or until the pastry is crisp.

☐ Remove the tart from the oven, cover loosely in foil to retain its heat and set aside. Move the potatoes to the top shelf of the oven and increase the temperature to 220C/gas 7. Continue roasting the potatoes for a further 25–30 minutes until golden and crisp.

☐ For the gravy, heat the oil and redcurrant jelly in a small saucepan, stirring until melted and smooth. Add the hot stock, bring to a simmer and stir in the cornflour. Simmer gently and stir continuously until you have the desired consistency. Set aside.

☐ Finally, cut the wild mushrooms into pieces, roughly chop the remaining chestnuts and finely chop the parsley. Heat the garlic oil in a heavy-based frying pan until hot, add the mushrooms and fry gently until softened. Stir in the chestnuts, cranberries and parsley and spoon over the tart to form a decorative layer. Reheat the gravy and serve with the tart and roast potatoes.

Persian Squash & Pistachio Roast

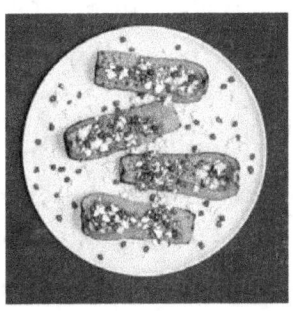

Serves: 6-8 Level: Easy Persian squash & pistachio roast ☐ 2 medium free-range eggs, (or to make it ☐ 400g squash olive oil

vegan, 2 tablespoons of chia seeds mixed

Persian squash & pistachio
☐ 2 cloves of garlic ☐ 1 pomegranate roast

☐ 50g dried apricots ☐ TOMATO SAUCE
☐ 50g sour cherries or cranberries ☐ 2 cloves of garlic
☐ 2 teaspoons cumin seeds ☐ 1 small onion
☐ 2 teaspoons coriander seeds ☐ 2 fresh red chilies
☐ 1 lemon ☐ 1 stick of cinnamon
☐ 1 bunch of fresh coriander ☐ ½ a bunch of fresh thyme

- ☐ 200 g tinned chestnuts ☐ 1 pinch of turmeric
- ☐ ½ teaspoon ground turmeric ☐ 2 x 400 g tins of plum tomatoes
- ☐ 1 teaspoon cinnamon ☐ 1 tablespoon balsamic vinegar
- ☐ 100g shelled pistachios ☐ FETA (OPTIONAL)
- ☐ 100g almonds ☐ 200g feta cheese, optional
- ☐ 100g cooked quinoa or brown rice ☐ 1 lemon, optional

☐ 2 medium free-range eggs ☐ (or 1 teaspoon coriander seeds optional to make it vegan, 2 tablespoons of chia seeds mixed with 6 tablespoons of water and

left to soak)
☐ 1 pomegranate

19
directions:

☐ Preheat the oven to 180°C/gas 4. Grease a 24cm loose bottomed tart tin with a little olive oil.
☐ Peel, deseed and chop the squash into 1cm chunks, then toss onto a baking tray with a drizzle of oil and sea salt and black pepper, and roast for 20 to 25 minutes.

☐ Peel and roughly chop the onion and garlic, and roughly chop the apricots and cranberries. Bash the cumin and coriander seeds, and zest the lemon. Pick and roughly chop the coriander, then roughly chop the chestnuts.

☐ In a frying pan over a medium heat, cook the onion in a little oil for 10 minutes or until soft and sweet. Add the garlic and cook for another minute, until beginning to soften, then add all the spices and a little more oil. Remove from the heat and set aside.

☐ Blitz the pistachios and almonds until they're ground to a coarse powder with a little texture. Tip into a bowl with the quinoa/rice and dried fruit, then add the lemon zest, coriander and chestnuts. Beat and stir in the eggs (or chia seed mix) and the onion.

☐ Take the squash out of the oven and mash half of it with the back of a fork, leaving the other half in chunks, then stir this into the mixture too.
☐ Pile the lot into the prepared tin and press down to flatten. Cook in the oven for 45 to 50 minutes, or until set.

☐ While it's cooking, make the tomato sauce. Peel and chop the garlic and onion. Place a large saucepan over a medium heat. Prick the chilies and add to the pan with a little oil, the cinnamon stick, sprigs of thyme, garlic, onion and turmeric.

☐ Cook for a minute or two, then add the plum tomatoes. Fill the tin with water and pour that in too, stirring to break up the tomatoes. Season with salt, stir through the balsamic vinegar and bring to the boil. Reduce the heat and simmer for 20 minutes.

☐ If using the feta, place it in a bowl, zest over the lemon, add the coriander seeds, some black pepper and a good drizzle of oil and leave it to marinate.
☐ Once the sauce is thick and glossy, pick out the chili, cinnamon and thyme. Set aside.
☐ Take the nut roast out of the oven, then carefully remove it from the tin and place it on a serving platter.

20
☐ Scatter the loaf with the feta (if using), and the pomegranate

seeds. Serve with the sauce in a side bowl.

Prime Rib

Serves: 12 Level: Easy

ingredients:

☐ 1 (10 pound) prime rib roast

☐ 6 cloves garlic, sliced
☐ salt and ground black pepper to taste
☐ 1/2 cup Dijon mustard

Recipies
directions:

☐ Preheat the oven to 500 degrees F (260 degrees C).

☐ Make slits all over the roast by pricking with a small knife. Insert slivers of sliced garlic. Season the roast with salt and pepper, then spread generously with mustard. Place on a rack in a roasting pan, and cover.

☐ Roast for 60 minutes in the preheated oven. Turn off oven. Leave oven closed, and do not peek for 90 minutes. The internal temperature of the meat should be at least 140 degrees F (60 degrees C) for medium-rare, or 155 degrees F (68 degrees C) for medium.

Christmas Recipies

Cauliflower & Broccoli Cheese

Serves: 8 Level: Easy

ingredients:

- [ ] 2 cloves of garlic

- [ ] 50g unsalted butter
- [ ] 50g plain flour
- [ ] 500ml semi-skimmed milk
- [ ] 500g fresh or frozen broccoli
- [ ] 75g mature cheddar cheese
- [ ] 1kg fresh or frozen cauliflower
- [ ] 2 slices of ciabatta or stale bread

- ☐ 2 sprigs of fresh thyme
- ☐ 25g flaked almonds
- ☐ olive oil

Recipies
directions:

- ☐ Preheat the oven to 180°C/350°F/gas 4.
- ☐ Peel and finely slice the garlic and put it into a medium pan on a medium heat with the butter.

- ☐ When the butter has melted, stir in the flour for a minute to make a paste, then gradually add the milk, whisking as you go, until lovely and smooth.

- ☐ Add the broccoli (cut up first, if using fresh) and simmer for around 20 minutes, or until the broccoli is cooked through and starts to break down, then mash or blitz with a stick blender (adding an extra splash of milk to loosen, if using fresh broccoli).

- ☐ Grate in half the Cheddar and season to perfection.

- ☐ Arrange the cauliflower in an appropriately sized baking dish (cut into florets first, if using fresh), pour over the broccoli white sauce and grate over the remaining Cheddar. Blitz the bread into breadcrumbs in a food processor, then pulse in the thyme leaves and almonds. Toss with a lug of oil and a pinch of salt and pepper, then scatter evenly over the cauliflower cheese.

- ☐ Bake for 1 hour, or until golden and cooked through, then enjoy!

Maple Roast Turkey And Gravy

Serves:20 Level: Medium

- ☐ 2 cups apple cider
- ☐ 1/3 cup real maple syrup
- ☐ 2 tablespoons chopped fresh thyme
- ☐ 2 tablespoons chopped fresh marjoram
- ☐ 2 1/2 teaspoons grated lemon zest
- ☐ 3/4 cup butter salt and ground black pepper to taste
- ☐ 14 pounds whole turkey, neck and giblets reserved
- ☐ 2 cups chopped onion 1 cup chopped celery
- ☐ 1 cup coarsely chopped carrots 2 cups chicken stock
- ☐ 3 tablespoons all-purpose flour 1 teaspoon chopped fresh thyme
- ☐ 1 bay leaf
- ☐ 2 tablespoons apple brandy (optional)

directions:

- ☐ Boil apple cider and maple syrup in a heavy saucepan over medium-high heat until reduced to 1/2 cup (about 20 minutes). Remove from heat and mix in 1/2 of the thyme and marjoram and all of the lemon zest. Add the butter, and whisk until melted. Add salt and ground pepper to taste. Cover and refrigerate until cold (syrup can be made up to 2 days ahead).

☐ Preheat oven to 375 degrees F (190 degrees C). Place oven rack in the lowest third of oven.

☐ Wash and dry turkey, and place in a large roasting pan. Slide hand under skin of the breast to loosen. Rub 1/2 cup of the maple butter mix under the breast skin. If planning on stuffing turkey, do so now. Rub 1/4 cup of the maple butter mixture over the outside of the turkey. With kitchen string, tie legs of turkey together loosely.

☐ Arrange the chopped onion, chopped celery, and chopped carrot around the turkey in the roasting pan. If desired, the neck and giblets may be added to the vegetables. Sprinkle the remaining thyme and marjoram over the vegetables, and pour the chicken stock into the pan.

☐ Roast turkey 30 minutes in the preheated oven. Reduce oven temperature to 350 degrees F (175 degrees C), and cover turkey loosely with foil. Continue to roast, about 3 to 4 hours unstuffed or 4 to 5 hours stuffed, until the internal temperature of the thigh reaches 180 degrees F (80 degrees C) and stuffing reaches 165 degrees F (75 degrees C). Transfer turkey to a platter, and cover with foil. Reserve pan mixture for gravy. Allow turkey to sit about 25 minutes before removing stuffing and carving.

☐ To Make Gravy: Strain pan juices into a measuring cup. Spoon fat from juices. Add enough chicken stock to make 3 cups. Transfer liquid to a heavy saucepan and bring to a boil. In a small bowl, mix reserved maple butter mixture with flour to form a paste, and whisk into the broth. Stir in thyme, bay leaf, and apple brandy. Boil until reduced and slightly thickened. Season with salt and pepper to taste.

Duck Breasts Stuffed With Sugared Nuts

Serves: 2 Level: Hard

- ☐ 2 x 160g duck breasts, skin on
- ☐ 2 shallots
- ☐ 50g white sugared almonds
- ☐ 7090 g unsalted butter
- ☐ 2 medium Desiree potatoes
- ☐ 100ml milk
- ☐ 1 pinch of ground nutmeg
- ☐ MARINADE
- ☐ 2 tablespoons sunny honey

- ☐ 1 tablespoons lowsalt soy sauce
- ☐ 50 g cognac
- ☐ 1 teaspoon ground cinnamon

directions:

- ☐ Start your duck a day ahead. Using a sharp knife, slash deep cuts through the skin, in a lattice pattern. Place the meat in a casserole dish and set aside.

For the marinade, mix the honey and soy sauce in a saucepan until combined, stir in the cognac and cinnamon and mix well. Place the pan over a medium heat and bring to a simmer, then remove from the heat after 2 minutes, allowing some of the alcohol to evaporate.

Drizzle over the duck, cover the dish with cling film and chill for 24 hours, turning the meat occasionally so that the marinade is distributed evenly.

The following day, preheat the oven to 170ºC/gas 3. Peel and finely chop the shallots, finely chop the sugared almonds and chop the butter into cubes.

Heat 40g of butter in a frying pan over a medium heat, add the chopped shallots and sauté for 8 minutes, until softened and beginning to caramelize, then remove from the heat and add the almonds.

Place a duck breast skin-side down, cover with the shallots and nuts, then top with the second breast, skin-side up. Wrap 3 or 4 pieces of kitchen string around the breasts, 3 to 4cm apart, securing with a knot. Set aside.

For the purée, put the unpeeled potatoes in a large pan of cold salted water over a high heat and bring to the boil. Cook for 20 to 30 minutes, or until you can easily insert a knife into them.

Meanwhile, put the duck parcel in a heavy-based, ovenproof frying pan over a low heat and cook for 5 minutes on each side, then place the pan in the oven for 6 minutes, to give perfectly rare meat (8 minutes for medium). Take the duck out of the pan, cover and leave to rest.

When they're ready, drain the potatoes and set aside to cool a bit. Peel while they're still warm, then mash into a fine purée.

Transfer to a saucepan and cook, stirring often, over a medium heat for 5 minutes, before gradually introducing the remaining cold butter, mixing well with a spatula until combined. Set aside.

In a separate pan, bring the milk to the boil over a medium heat, add a pinch of nutmeg, then stir into the potato mixture until absorbed.
Cut the strings on the duck, carve into thick slices and serve with the puréed potatoes on the side.

Honey Glazed Ham

Serves: 15 Level: Easy

ingredients:

☐ 1 (5 pound) ready-to-eat ham

☐ 1/4 cup whole cloves
☐ 1/4 cup dark corn syrup
☐ 2 cups honey

directions:

☐ Preheat oven to 325 degrees F (165 degrees C). Christmas Recipies

☐ Score ham, and stud with the whole cloves. Place ham in foil lined pan.
☐ In the top half of a double boiler, heat the corn syrup, honey and butter. Keep glaze warm while baking ham.

☐ Brush glaze over ham, and bke for 1 hour and 15 minutes in the preheated oven. Baste ham every 10 to 15 minutes with the honey glaze. During the last 4 to 5 minutes of baking, turn on broiler to caramelize the glaze.

☐ Remove from oven, and let sit a few minutes before serving.

Christmas Tortellini & Spinach Soup

Serves: 14 Level: Easy

☐ 2 cans (14 1/2 ounces each) vegetable broth
☐ 1 package (9 ounces) refrigerated cheese tortellini or tortellini of your choice
☐ 1 can (15 ounces) white kidney or cannellini beans, rinsed and drained
☐ 1 can (14 1/2 ounces) Italian diced tomatoes, undrained
☐ 1/4 teaspoon salt
☐ 1/8 teaspoon pepper
☐ 3 cups fresh baby spinach
☐ 3 tablespoons minced fresh basil
☐ 1/4 cup shredded Asiago cheese

directions:
Christmas Recipies

☐ In a large saucepan, bring broth to a boil. Add tortellini; reduce heat. Simmer, uncovered, for 5 minutes.

☐ Stir in the beans, tomatoes, salt and pepper; return to a simmer.
☐ Cook 45 minutes longer or until tortellini are tender.
☐ Stir in spinach and basil,cook until spinach is wilted. Top servings with cheese.
Recipies ingredients:

Christmas Eve Confetti Pasta

Serves: 8 Level: Easy

☐ 1 package (16 ounces) linguine
☐ 1 cup chopped sweet red pepper
☐ 1 cup chopped green pepper
☐ 1/3 cup chopped onio
☐ 3 garlic cloves, peeled and thinly sliced
☐ 1/4 teaspoon salt
☐ 1/4 teaspoon dried oregano
☐ 1/8 teaspoon crushed red pepper flakes
☐ 1/8 teaspoon pepper
☐ 1/4 cup olive oil
☐ 2 pounds cooked small shrimp, peeled and deveined

☐ 1/2 cup shredded Parmesan cheese
directions:
Christmas Recipies

☐ Cook linguine according to package directions. Meanwhile, in a Dutch oven, saute the peppers, onion, garlic and seasonings in oil until vegetables are tender.

☐ Add the shrimp; cook and stir 23 minutes longer or until heated through. Drain linguine; toss with shrimp mixture. Sprinkle with cheese.

Recipies

ingredients:

Chicken Wild Rice Soup

Serves: 14 Level: Medium

- [ ] 2 quarts chicken broth
- [ ] 1/2 pound fresh mushrooms, chopped
- [ ] 1 cup finely chopped celery
- [ ] 1 cup shredded carrots
- [ ] 1/2 cup finely chopped onion
- [ ] 1 teaspoon chicken bouillon granules
- [ ] 1 teaspoon dried parsley flakes
- [ ] 1/4 teaspoon garlic powder
- [ ] 1/4 teaspoon dried thyme
- [ ] 1/4 cup butter, cubed
- [ ] 1/4 cup all-purpose flour
- [ ] 1 can (10 3/4 ounces) condensed cream of mushroom soup, undiluted
- [ ] 1/2 cup dry white wine or additional chicken broth
- [ ] 3 cups cooked wild rice
- [ ] 2 cups cubed cooked chicken

Recipies

☐ In a large saucepan, combine the first nine ingredients. Bring to a directions:

boil. Reduce heat; cover and simmer for 30 minutes.

☐ In Dutch oven, melt butter; stir in flour until smooth. Gradually whisk in broth mixture. Bring to a boil; cook and stir for 2 minutes or until thickened. Whisk in soup and wine. Add rice and chicken; heat through.

Creamy Seafood-Stuffed Shells

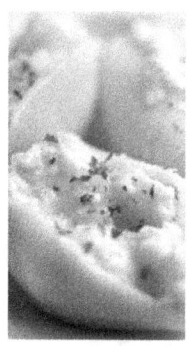

Serves: 8 Level: Medium

- ☐ 24 uncooked jumbo pasta shells
- ☐ 1 tablespoon finely chopped green pepper
- ☐ 1 tablespoon chopped red onion
- ☐ 1 teaspoon plus 1/4 cup butter, divided
- ☐ 2 cans (6 ounces each) lump crabmeat, drained
- ☐ 1 package (5 ounces) frozen cooked salad shrimp, thawed
- ☐ 1 large egg, lightly beaten

- ☐ 1/2 cup shredded part-skim mozzarella cheese
- ☐ 1/4 cup mayonnaise
- ☐ 2 tablespoons plus 4 cups 2% milk, divided
- ☐ 1 1/2 teaspoons seafood seasoning, divided
- ☐ 1/4 teaspoon pepper
- ☐ 1/4 cup all-purpose flour
- ☐ 1/4 teaspoon coarsely ground pepper
- ☐ 1 1/2 cups grated Parmesan cheese

directions:

☐ Cook pasta according to package directions.
☐ Meanwhile, in a small skillet, sauté green pepper and onion in 1 teaspoon butter until tender; set aside.

☐ In a large bowl, combine crab, shrimp, egg, mozzarella cheese, mayonnaise, 2 tablespoons milk, 1 teaspoon seafood seasoning, pepper and green pepper mixture.

☐ Preheat oven to 350°. Drain and rinse pasta; stuff each shell with 1 rounded tablespoon of seafood mixture. Place in a greased 13x9-in. baking dish.

☐ In a small saucepan, melt remaining butter over medium heat. Whisk in flour and coarsely ground pepper; gradually whisk in remaining milk. Bring to a boil; cook and stir 2 minutes or until thickened. Stir in Parmesan cheese.

☐ Pour over stuffed shells. Sprinkle with remaining seafood seasoning. Bake, uncovered, 30-35 minutes or until bubbly. Yield: 8 servings.

Ultimate Roast Chicken

Serves: 6 Level: Medium

- ☐ 1 x 4 kg free-range chicken, with giblets
- ☐ Few sprigs of fresh thyme
- ☐ Few sprigs of fresh rosemary
- ☐ few sprigs of fresh sage
- ☐ 2 onions
- ☐ 2 carrots
- ☐ 2 sticks of celery
- ☐ 4 fresh bay leaves
- ☐ 1 bulb of garlic
- ☐ 500 g free range chicken wings
- ☐ olive oil
- ☐ 2 heaped tablespoons plain flour
- ☐ 150 ml white wine
- ☐ 1 liter organic chicken stock
- ☐ FLAVOURED BUTTER
- ☐ 75 g dried porcini
- ☐ 25 g unsalted butter , (at room temperature)
- ☐ 2 lemons

☐ 1 whole nutmeg, for grating
☐ 3 cloves of garlic
☐ ½ a bunch of fresh thyme
9 slices of higher-welfare pancetta ☐ Preheat the oven to 190ºC/gas 5. Leave the chicken to room temperature while you make your butter.

directions:

☐ Pop the dried porcini into a small bowl, cover with boiling water and allow to sit for 5 minutes, then use a slotted spoon to remove the mushrooms, and reserve both them and their soaking liquid.

☐ Put the butter into a bowl and finely grate in the lemon zest (reserve the lemons for later) and half of the nutmeg, then peel and crush in the garlic.

☐ Pick in the thyme leaves, chop and add the pancetta, then add the soaked porcini along with a pinch of sea salt and black pepper.

☐ Mix everything into the butter until combined, then divide into two. Set aside in the fridge until needed.

☐ Take the chicken and use your fingers and a spatula to gently work your way between the skin and the meat. Start at the side of the cavity just above the leg and work gently up along the breastbone, towards the back, until you create a large cavity.

☐ Poke half of the butter into it, using your hands to push it through the skin right to the back, so it coats the breast meat as evenly as possible. Do the same on the other side with the remaining butter, and if there's any left, rub it over the outside of the bird.

☐ Halve the reserved zested lemons and pop in the cavity of the chicken along with the thyme, rosemary and sage sprigs – this will add extra flavor while the chicken cooks.
☐ Peel and halve the onions, peel and roughly chop the carrots, then trim and roughly chop the celery.
☐ Pile the veg into a large roasting tray, smash and add the whole garlic cloves along with the bay leaves and chicken wings, then drizzle with oil.
☐ Place your whole chicken on top, drizzle with oil and season with salt and pepper.

☐ Roast the chicken in the oven for about 2 hours, or until the skin is golden and crispy and the juices run clear when the thigh is pierced with a sharp knife, basting twice during cooking. If the vegetables start looking dry, add a splash of water to the tray to stop them burning.

☐ Remove the tray from the oven and transfer the chicken to a board. Cover with a sheet of tin foil and a tea towel

40 and leave to rest for 15 minutes.
☐ To prepare the gravy, spoon away any excess fat from the mixture in the roasting tray, then place on the hob over

Italian Style Pizza

Serves: 2 pizzas Level: Easy

ingredients:

- 2 prebaked mini pizza crusts

- 1/2 cup prepared pesto
- 2/3 cup shredded part-skim mozzarella cheese
- 1/2 cup sliced sweet onion
- 1/2 cup thinly sliced fresh mushrooms
- 1/4 cup roasted sweet red peppers, drained
- 2 tablespoons grated Parmesan cheese

- Place crusts on an ungreased baking sheet; spread with pesto.

directions:
- Layer with mozzarella cheese, onion, mushrooms and peppers; sprinkle with Parmesan cheese.
- Bake at 400° for 10-12 minutes or until cheese is melted.

ingredients:
Recipies

Mexican Sweetcorn Pancakes, Poached Eggs And Salsa

Serves: 2 Level: Medium

- [ ] For the sweetcorn pancakes
- [ ] 100g/3½oz plain flour
- [ ] 1 tsp baking powder
- [ ] 1 free-range egg
- [ ] 150ml/5fl oz whole milk
- [ ] salt and freshly ground black pepper
- [ ] 1 sweetcorn on the cob, kernels only
- [ ] 1 tbsp vegetable oil
- [ ] For the tomato chilli salsa
- [ ] 3 tomatoes, skin and seeds removed, chopped
- [ ] 6 coriander sprigs, leaves only, chopped
- [ ] 1 green chilli, very finely chopped
- [ ] pinch sugar
- [ ] ¼ small red onion, finely chopped
- [ ] 1 lime, juice only
- [ ] pinch sea salt

- ☐ freshly ground black pepper
- ☐ For the poached eggs
- ☐ 1 tbsp white wine vinegar

4 free-range eggs

directions:

☐ For the sweetcorn pancakes, sieve the flour and baking powder into a mixing bowl, then whisk in the egg and half of the milk to form a thick batter with a consistency slightly thicker than double cream. Add more milk as necessary to loosen the mixture. Season to taste with salt and freshly ground black pepper, then stir in the sweetcorn.

☐ Heat the oil in a frying pan over a medium to high heat. Spoon half of the batter into the pan and fry for 1-2 minutes on each side, or until the pancake is golden-brown on both sides. Set the pancake aside on a warm plate and cover loosely with aluminum foil. Repeat with the remaining batter.

☐ For the tomato chili salsa, mix the tomatoes, coriander, chili, sugar, finely chopped onion, lime juice and salt until well combined. Season to taste with freshly ground black pepper.

☐ For the poached eggs, bring a pan of water to the boil, stir in the vinegar and turn down the heat so that the water is simmering. Add the eggs and poach for 3-4 minutes, or until cooked to your liking, then remove from the pan with a slotted spoon and drain on kitchen paper.

☐ To serve, place one of the sweetcorn pancakes onto each plate, arrange two of the poached eggs on top, and finish with a spoonful of the tomato chili salsa.

Mushroom Purses

Serves: 4 Level: Easy

ingredients:

☐ 4 tbsp olive oil, plus extra for the pastry
☐ 3 garlic cloves, finely chopped
☐ 1.2kg/2lb 7oz wild mushrooms, larger mushrooms chopped
☐ 3 tbsp coarsely chopped parsley
☐ 1 small chilli, finely chopped (optional)
☐ 8 rectangles readymade filo pastry, about 20x20cm/8x8in
small bunch fresh chives
Recipies
☐ Preheat the oven to 220C/450F/Gas 8.

directions: ☐ Heat the oil in a frying pan, add the garlic and mushrooms and fry over a high heat for 3-4 minutes, or until just cooked. Season with salt and freshly ground black pepper and sprinkle over the parsley. Set aside to cool.

☐ Brush one side of each sheet of filo pastry all over with a little olive oil.

☐ Place one sheet of filo pastry on top of another to create two layers of pastry, then spoon a quarter of the mushroom mixture into the center of the pastry.

☐ Gather up the corners of the pastry to create a parcel and secure with a couple of chives. Brush all over with olive oil and place onto a baking tray.

☐ Repeat the process with the remaining filo pastry and mushroom mixture.

☐ Bake the parcels fo 10-12 minutes, or until the pastry is cooked through and golden-brown.

Cakes & Bakery

Gingerbread Men

Serves: 8 Level: Easy

- ☐ 1 (3.5 ounce) package cook and serve butterscotch pudding mix
- ☐ 1/2 cup butter
- ☐ 1/2 cup packed brown sugar
- ☐ 1 egg
- ☐ 1 1/2 cups all-purpose flour
- ☐ 1/2 teaspoon baking soda
- ☐ 1 1/2 teaspoons ground ginger
- ☐ 1 teaspoon ground cinnamon

Christmas Recipies

- ☐ In a medium bowl, cream together the dry butterscotch pudding mix, butter, and brown sugar until smooth. Stir in the egg. Combine directions:

the flour, baking soda, ginger, and cinnamon; add to the pudding mixture. Cover, and chill dough until firm, about 1 hour.

- ☐ Preheat the oven to 350 degrees F (175 degrees C). Grease baking sheets. On a floured board, roll dough out to about 1/8 inch thickness, and cut into man shapes using a cookie cutter. Place cookies 2 inches apart on the prepared baking sheets.

☐ Bake for 10 to 12 minutes in the preheated oven, until cookies are golden at the edges. Cool on wire racks.

ingredients:
Recipies

Stollen Muffins

Serves: 10 Level: Medium

- [ ] 200g plain flour
- [ ] 50g ground almonds
- [ ] 1 tsp baking powder
- [ ] 1 tsp bicarbonate of soda
- [ ] ½ tsp ground cinnamon
- [ ] 100g golden caster sugar
- [ ] 100g marzipan diced
- [ ] 25g pistachios, roughly chopped
- [ ] 50g toasted flaked almonds
- [ ] 25g sultanas or raisins
- [ ] 50g dried cherries or cranberries
- [ ] 50g dried apricots, diced
- [ ] 2 large eggs
- [ ] 100g unsalted butter, melted and cooled
- [ ] 125ml full fat natural yogurt
- [ ] 1 tsp almond extract

- [ ] 2 tbsp icing sugar
- [ ] 12 paper muffin cases (we used tulip cases)

Christmas Recipies

- [ ] Heat oven to 220C/200C fan/gas 7 and put the muffin cases in a 12-hole

directions:

muffin tin.

- [ ] Mix the flour, ground almonds, baking powder, bicarb, 1/4 tsp cinnamon, the sugar, marzipan, nuts and dried fruit in a mixing bowl.

- [ ] Whisk together the eggs, melted butter, yogurt and almond extract, then pour over the dry ingredients and very quickly mix with a wooden spoon until the mixture has just come together – the most important thing is to not overmix – don't worry if there are still a few floury bits.

- [ ] Divide the mix between the cases and put in the oven on the top shelf. Bake for 5 mins, then lower the heat to 180C/160C fan/gas 4 and bake for 15 mins more until they are risen, golden, and a skewer inserted into the middle of them comes out clean.

- [ ] Once they have cooled a little and are firm enough to handle, lift out of the tin onto wire racks and cool for 5 mins.
- [ ] Mix the icing sugar with the remaining 1/4 tsp cinnamon and sieve over the muffins.
- [ ] Serve warm. Will keep for 4 days in an airtight container.

Homemade Crumpets With Burnt Honey Butter

Serves:4 Level: Hard

- ☐ 250ml milk
- ☐ 200g plain flour
- ☐ 1 tsp fastaction dried yeast
- ☐ 1 tsp golden caster sugar
- ☐ 2 tbsp vegetable oil, plus extra for greasing
- ☐ For the burnt honey butter
- ☐ 5 tbsp clear honey
- ☐ 140g unsalted butter, at room temperature ☐

directions:

Christmas Recipies

Slowly heat the milk in a small pan until it starts to bubble around the edges, then leave it to cool. Put the flour, yeast, sugar and ½ tsp fine salt in a large bowl, and gradually mix in the cooled milk to make a smooth, loose batter. Cover and leave to rise in a warm place for 1hr1hr 30 mins or until doubled in size and very bubbly.

☐ Meanwhile, make the honey butter. Heat the honey in a small saucepan over a medium

high heat. Let it bubble until it turns to a deep gold, then remove and cool slightly. Using electric beaters or, beat the butter in a large bowl until fluffy and pale, add a large pinch of sea salt, then fold in the warm honey. Scrape into a serving bowl and chill. Can be made a day ahead.

☐ Once the batter has risen, heat the grill to high. Gently grease the insides of 5 x 9cm metal cooks' rings with oil. Heat a large frying pan over the medium heat, add 1 tbsp oil and put the rings in the pan.
☐ Spoon the batter into the rings until they are half full. Let the crumpets cook slowly for about 10 mins or until the mixture has set and the bubbles on top have all popped. Lift the rings away carefully.
☐ Grill the crumpets in the pan for 710 mins or until the tops are golden brown.
☐ Warm through in an oven at 140C/120C fan/gas 1 if you've made them in advance. Repeat with the remaining mix, then serve with the burnt honey butter.

Candy Cane Cookies

Serves: 25 Cookies Level: Easy

ingredients:

☐ 1 box sugar cookie mix

☐ 1/2 stick butter, melted
☐ 1 egg
☐ 1/3 cup softened cream cheese
☐ 1/2 cup all-purpose flour, plus additional for surface
☐ Red food coloring
☐ 1 1/2 teaspoons peppermint extract

directions:

☐ Preheat oven to 325 degrees F.

☐ In a bowl, combine sugar cookie mix, melted butter, egg, cream cheese, and flour; mix together to form dough. Separate dough into 2 equal portions and place in 2 different bowls. Add red food coloring gradually to 1 bowl of dough, kneading together until desired shade of red is created.

☐ Take another bowl of uncolored dough, add peppermint extract and knead together. On a floured work surface, shape each dough into balls and then roll each ball into 1/4-inch-wide ropes, each about 6 inches long. For each cookie, carefully twist some of the red and white ropes of dough together and shape into a candy cane.

☐ Spread candy canes out on cookie sheets and bake on the top shelf of the oven for about 10 to 12 minutes. Transfer to a rack to cool before serving.

www.ingramcontent.com/pod-product-compliance
Lightning Source LLC
Chambersburg PA
CBHW071442070526
44578CB00001B/196